The Fictional World of Gabriel Garcia Marquez

The Fictional World of Gabriel Garcia Marquez

Santwana Haldar

Prestige Books International
New Delhi

Published by
Prestige Books International
New Delhi 110 060
email: prestigebooks@gmail.com

ISBN: 978-93-82186-57-1

Printed in India

Contents

Preface
9

Gabriel Garcia Marquez:
A Brief Bio-Sketch
11

Latin American Short Story and Gabriel Garcia Marquez
20

History, Mundane Reality and Fantasy in Marquez's Fiction
52

Solitude, Solidarity and Love in
Marquez's Fiction
97

Garcia Marquez's Social Concerns and his Journalistic Zeal
141

Appendix
The Art of Garcia Marquez and
(Magic) Realism
176

Bibliography
183

For

Jyoti

& also for

Pramiti

When she will grow up

Acknowledgements

Grateful acknowledgement is made to the following periodicals and anthology in which parts of this book were first published:

Journal of the Odisha Association for English Studies (ISSN 2249-6726)
The Atlantic Literary Review Quarterly (ISSN 0972-3269)
Ten Nobel Laureates, IMAGE (BBSR)

Preface

Gabriel Garcia Marquez (1928-2014), the Colombian journalist and writer of fiction, was awarded the Nobel Prize for Literature in 1982. After the publication of his celebrated novel *Cien Anos de Soredad* in 1967 he became famous overnight and the English translation of the original Spanish by Gregory Rabassa *One Hundred Years of Solitude* (1970) brought him immediate fame throughout the world and the novel was accepted as a classic on the grandest scale. Since then all his books have been translated in almost all the languages of the world and Marquez has been universally accepted as the best chronicler of the national tragedy. Marquez was brought into the limelight as much for the theme of his fictional writings—he exposed the exact nature of Latin America's suffering during the postcolonial period, the devastations caused by dictatorship, corruption and Civil Wars—as for the novel technique he used for his fiction. He took up the challenge of facing the severe punishment imposed on him by the dictatorial rule while exposing the fact of massacre caused by the North American Fruit Company aided by the government force, the facts that had been erased from all records. He had to remain jobless and had to be exiled from his land for raising his voice against censorship. It was not any particular government that he opposed, but the system of governance that curbed individual freedom and inflicted torture on the marginalized. Surprisingly, his strong political view along with journalist's zeal to reveal the exact nature of what actually happened was combined with an artist's devotion to an innovative technique. He sincerely opposed the British tradition of realistic novel and embraced one based on folk tales, legends, popular beliefs and fantasy. Often described as 'magic realism,' this technique helped Marquez to bring together the multiple planes of reality in a harmonious way. To serve his purpose he uses multiple narrative voices and the fantasy appears as reality as it is presented from the perspective of the believer.

The present book discusses all the fictional writings of Garcia Marquez, including the stories. Through detailed analysis of the texts Marquez's views on history, contemporary socio-political reality and also on solitude and love have been expounded.

Santwana Haldar

Gabriel Garcia Marquez: A Brief Bio-Sketch

Gabriel Jose Garcia Marquez was born on March 6, 1928 in Aracataca, a small town in Northern Columbia by the Caribbean, where he was raised by his maternal grandparents. (Grazia Bordone was told by his press agent that the right year was 1927. *www.astro.com/astrodatabank/ Garcia_ Marquez_Gabriel*). His grandfather, Colonel Nicolas Ricardo Marquez Mejia, was a liberal veteran of the War of a Thousand days[1] and was considered to be hero in the locality. The Colonel had quite an intriguing life and was an excellent story teller who nourished the imagination of young Gabriel with his stories and also taught him lessons from history and life that left an everlasting mark on the boy. His grandmother, Tranquilina Iguaran Cotes, also influenced Gabriel, letting him enter into the world of superstitions and folk beliefs which was later modified and used in fiction by the great writer. Gabriel stayed with his grandparents till the death of his grandfather and then started living with his parents. His mother, Luisa Santiaga Marquez Igoaran, one of the two children born to the Colonel and his wife, married Gabriel Eligeo Garcia, a former medical student and a member of the Conservative party and a new settler in the town, against the will of her father who at last surrendered to the romantic tenacity of the couple. After the death of the Colonel when Gabriel was hardly eight or nine year old, he came to Sucre where his father was working as a pharmacist. His formal education started at that time and he was sent to a boarding school in Barranquilla, a port city at the mouth of Magdalena River.

In 1940, Gabriel was awarded a scholarship to a secondary school, the 'Liceo Nacional' in Zipaquira, a city thirty miles to the north of Bogota which was run by the Jesuits. The school was meant for gifted students, but at first Gabriel found it dismal and oppressing. Gradually he got used to the environment, being stimulated by his studies. Soon he received reputation as a writer among his companions, thanks to his reading aloud stories to his mates in the evening and his cartoons. In 1946, after graduation, he got enrolled in the 'Universidad Nacional' in Bogota as a law student, only to honor his parents' will. It was during this time that he met his future wife, Mercedes Barcha Pardo, then a thirteen-year-old girl of Egyptian origin. He had no mind in reading law and he engaged himself in reading literature. As he wrote in his memoir, during this time he had the opportunity to go through Kafka's 'Metamorphosis' and was inspired to write story on Kafka's model. His first story 'The Third Resignation' was published in 1946 in 'El Espectador.' He wrote ten more stories for the news papers over the next few years.

Gabriel Garcia Marquez's rise as a writer of fiction was closely related to his rise as a reporter and surprisingly, he treated the two different modes of writing with equal importance as well as depth of vision. His fictional writings were in many ways an extension of his journalistic writing in a new form, both revealing his humanistic feelings and a zeal for unearthing reality. His grandfather's close connection with the Liberal Party developed in him a natural sympathy for the Liberals and he took up pens to reveal the torture inflicted on the Liberals. The 1948 assassination of the Liberal leader Gaitan moved him so profoundly that he even participated in the riot of 'El Bagotazo,' having his own quarter partially burned down. He was then transferred to the 'Universidad de Cartagena' where he pursued law half-heartedly. He started writing a daily column for 'El Universal,' a Cartagena newspaper, and finally bade adieu to Law. He devoted himself totally to writing and moved to

Barranquilla. Over the next few years he started associating with a literary circle called 'el grupo de Barranquilla' and by this time he began to read Hemmingway, Joyce, Virginia Woolf and Faulkner. He also read classics like Sophocles' *Oedipus Rex* and was greatly influenced by these masters. In Faulkner's mythical 'Yeknopatawpha,' Marquez might have found the concept of Macondo, the mythical town used as backdrop in *One Hundred Years of Solitude* and other stories. His ideas of a plot revolving around society and the abuses of power might also be nurtured by *Oedipus Rex* and *Antigone.* By this time a very common incident took place that inspired him to write quite a new type of fiction. One day his mother called on him for the purpose of arranging the sale of his grandfather's house in Aracataca and he visited the haunted house accompanied by his mother. The visit evoked such a swirl of memories in his head that he was completely overwhelmed and found his mythical town Macondo (the word means banana in Bantu language) in his memory of Aracataca[2]. The imaginary locality was first used in his novella *Leaf Storm* (Spanish *La Hojarasca)* which was completed in an energetic rush of inspiration.

Marquez continued writing columns for newspapers with a steady job in the office of 'El Heraldo' where he worked during the day and in evening he worked on his fiction and talked with his friends. In 1953 he left the job, being seized by a sudden restlessness. He started selling encyclopedias in La Guajira with a friend. He travelled around a bit, and finally got engaged to Mercedes. In 1954, he moved back to Bogota and accepted a job on the staff of 'El Espectador' as a writer of stories and film reviews. In 1955 he got involved in a situation that led to his temporary exile from Colombia. There was a sensational news that a small Colombian destroyer 'Caldas' was swamped in high seas on its return to Cartagena and the only sailor Luis Alejandro Valasco who managed to survive for ten days clinging to a life raft on the sea was finally rescued and honored by the state for his heroic survival. There was a volcanic effect when it was published in 'El Espectador' that there was no storm and that 'Caldas' was overloaded with illegal cargo—Marquez was the reporter who recorded Valasco's confessions—as the government's export of illegal drugs was exposed. The sailor was tossed out of the Navy and fearing that Marquez might be prosecuted by the dictator Gustavo Rogas Pinilla, his editors sent him on assignment to Italy to over the imminent death of Pope Pius Twelfth. The Pope's unexpected survival made this assignment pointless and therefore Marquez now arranged to wander around Europe as a correspondent. After seven years of writing, his friends managed to publish *La Hojarasca* (*Leaf Storm*) in Bogota in 1955.

After travelling through Geneva, Rome, Poland and Hungary, Marquez finally came to Paris and found him jobless. The Pinilla government had shut down the press of 'El Espectador.' Struggling hard with poverty he stayed in the outskirt of Paris, this time engaged in writing fiction again. He wrote drafts of *No One Writes to the Colonel* and parts of 'This Town of Shit,' the book that was later published as *In Evil Hour.* He then travelled to London and fearing to enter Colombia, came to Venezuela, the chosen shelter of the Colombian refugees. In Venezuela he met his old friend Apuleyo Mendoza who was then an editor of 'Elite,' a Caracas newsweekly, and started working with him. They travelled throughout the communist countries of Europe, contributing articles to various Latin American publications. During this tour Marquez realized that Communism could be as terrible as 'la violencia.' After returning from the tour Mendoza began to work for 'Moments' and Marquez was also offered another job. In 1958, Marquez risked a visit to Colombia; he slipped into Barranquilla and married Mercedes who had been waiting for him and both of them slipped back to Caracas. The newly-wed couple had to face acute financial crisis as Marquez and also his friend Mendoza resigned because of the sudden pro-USA stance of 'Moments.' Marquez soon went to Havana in order to cover Castro revolution. He was so inspired by the revolution that he made contact with a Bogota branch of Castro's news agency 'Prensa Latina' and developed a long friendship with Castro.

In 1959, Marquez's first son Roderigo was born and the family moved to New York City where he supervised the North American branch of 'Prensa Latina.' He had to work under death threat from angry Americans. However, after a year he resigned his position as he was disillusioned by the ideological rifts occurring in Cuba's communist party. He then moved to Mexico City and started writing subtitles for films and worked on screenplays. During this time he published *El coronel no tiene quien le escriba* in 1961 (English translation *No One Writes to the Colonel*) and *Los funerals de la Mama Grande* in 1962 (English translation *Big Mama's Funeral*). In 1962 his second son Gonzalo was born and *In Evil Hour* (Spanish *La Mala Hora*) was also published. His friends convinced him to enter it into Colombian Esso literary contest in Bogota. Marquez rewrote the story and gave a new title *La Mala Hara* in lieu of the original *Esto Pueblo de mierla* (The Town of Shit) and won the contest. The next few years he hardly wrote anything except a film script co-written with Cartos Fuentes. A sudden inspiration overpowered him in 1965 and he started writing his masterpiece *Cien Anos de Soledad* which was published in 1967 and its English version *One Hundred Years of Solitude* (translated by Gregory Rabbasa) was published in 1970. Marquez kept him confined in a room while composing the novel, putting Mercedes in charge of the family. He wrote everyday for eighteen months, hardly keeping any contact with the outer world. It was Mercedes who sold and pawned all the household articles to feed the family and to supply the author with rims of papers and tins of cigarettes. His friends came in support and he humbly remembers their help in his memoir. At last the long awaited book was published in June 1967 and within a week 8000 copies were sold. It was soon translated from Spanish into other languages including English, contributing to Marquez's worldwide fame. *Innocent Erendira and Other Stories* was published in 1972 and in 1973 he put out a collection of his journalistic works *When I was Happy and Uninformed.* After the assassination of Chile's president Salvador Allende in 1973 Marquez decided to take more active role in politics. He founded a left-wing magazine 'Alternative' in Bogota and participated in the Russell Tribunal to get the human rights abuses in Latin America published. The success of *One Hundred Years of Solitude* increased the expectations of all and most of the critics were disappointed with the labyrinthine movement and lengthy sentences of *El Otono del Ptriarcha* published in 1975 (English translation by Gregory Rabassa *Autumn of the Patriarch* was published in 1976). Later, however, the novel has been appreciated as a work of shifting realities.

After Marquez became financially well off, he began to spend money for social and political causes. He supported leftist causes in Colombia, Venezuela, Nicaragua, Argentina and Angola. He helped found and then supported HABEAS, an organization dedicated to correcting the abuses of Latin American power and freeing political prisoners. In 1981, his novel *Chronicle of a Death Foretold* (Spanish *Cronica de una muerte anunciada*) in which a murder that had happened twenty seven years before was reconstructed was published. This year the Conservative government of Colombia accused him of financing the M-19, a Liberal group of Guerrillas. He received political asylum in Mexico and was staying there when he was declared the Nobel Laureate for literature in 1982. In 1981 he was also awarded the French Legion of Honor, the highest honor that France gives to a foreigner. The Colombian government was widely criticized for taking action against the son of the soil who was the first Nobel Laureate of Colombia and also brought other rare honor to his country. However, the new elected president of Colombia invited him back and Marquez spent his last life both in Colombia and in Mexico City. He used the money he received from his Nobel Prize to start a daily newspaper in Colombia. In 1982 he wrote a screenplay about Sandinistas and the Nicaraguan Revolution. His next novel *Love in the Time of Cholera* (Spanish *El amor en los tiempos del colera* published in 1985 and the English translation by Edith Grossman in 1988) has hardly anything to do with politics, though the backdrop of civil war looms large. It is a non-traditional love story that depicts the romantic love of two young persons which was proved to be hopeless after the girl rebuffed her lover and married an established doctor and which was materialized when the doctor died after fifty-one years, nine months and four days. *The General in his Labyrinth* (translated by Edith Grossman) was published in 1990, *Strange Pilgrims,* a collection of stories translated by Edith Grossman (Spanish *Doce cuentos peregrines*) in 1992, and his *Of Love and Other Demons* (Spanish *Del amor Y otros demonios* and English translation by Edith Grossman) in 1994. The much adored novel was followed in 1996 by a journalistic work *News of Kidnapping* that gives details of the atrocities of the Colombian Drug trade. This return to journalism was emphasized in 1999 when he purchased a struggling Colombian magazine *Cambio* and was a prodigious contributor to it as long as he was able to type, for he was soon diagnosed with lymphatic cancer and his activities had to be limited.

The disease could not however dominate Marquez's creative spirit. In 2002 he published the first of a projected three-volume autobiography *Vivir para contaria.* Edith Grossman's English translation *Living to Tell the Tale* was published in 2003. In October 2004, a new novel *Memoria de mis putas tristes* (translated by Edith Grossman as *Memories of My Melancholy Whores),* the romance of a ninety year old man and a pubescent concubine, was published and created sensation all over the world. One of the most fascinating authors in any language, Gabriel Garcia Marquez breathed his last on 17th April, 2014. All his fiction and non-fiction writings, except however some of his purely journalistic writings, were translated into all the important languages all over the world and he is one of the few writers who are both seriously discussed and adored in all the languages he has been translated. He will be remembered as a master of short story, a journalist who staked his life and property for the cause of revealing the truth, an innovator of new techniques of novel, a magician of words and also a key essayist. But above all, he was a humanist whose indomitable spirit could not take rest until the atrocities inflicted on helpless persons by the cruel and powerful state machinery could be released. And it did not much matter for him which medium he used for his goal; it could be fiction or journalism or even cinema. Perhaps he was the only successful writer who could freely use fiction, journalism and cinema for delivering an abiding statement on human condition.

Notes

1 Colombia declared itself independent from Spain when Napoleon ousted the Spanish king in 1810. But this independence hardly brought peace in Colombia. It was quickly occupied in 1815, though Simon Bolivar freed it soon in 1820 and became its first president. In 1849, the country was apparently advanced with the formation of two political parties, the Liberals and the Conservatives, based on two different ideologies. But in actuality the two parties behaved as two warring clans, both being corrupt and repressive. The country was also split into two main regional groups—the 'costenos' of the coastal Caribbean and the 'cachacos' of the central highland. Traditionally, the tropical Caribbean coast was the land of the Liberals and the cool mountains and villages of the interior was the place of the Conservatives who took pride in being aristocratic and racially pure as well as able to speak excellent Spanish. Throughout the nineteenth century Colombia

experienced civil wars and in 1899, the century of bloodshed had its culmination when the War of a Thousand Days started. It was Colombia's most devastating civil war, a conflict that ended in 1902 with the defeat of the Liberals. The war claimed the lives of over one lakh people, mostly peasants and their sons. Marquez's grandfather fought in this war.

2 In his autobiography Marquez explains his fascination with the word and concept of Macondo. He describes a trip back to Aracataca as a young man, "The train stopped at a station that had no town, and a short while later it passed the only banana plantation along the route that had its name written over the gate: Macondo. This word had attracted my attention ever since the first trip I had made with my grandfather, but I discovered only as an adult that I liked its poetic resonance. I never heard anyone say it and did not even ask myself what it meant. . .I happened to read in an encyclopedia that it is a tropical tree resembling to 'ceiba' (2003;19).

Latin American Short Story and Gabriel Garcia Marquez

Latin American literature[1] has a rich history and the wealth of its short story is excellent. Among others there are Ricardo Palma, Machado de Assis, Jorge Luis Borges, Horacio Quiroga, Juan Jose Arreola, Alejo Carpentier, Miguel Angel Asturias, Julio Cortazar, Mario Vargas Llosa and Gabriel Garcia Marquez whose contribution to short story made it a major genre enjoying popularity as well as genuine recognitions in the literary circles all over the world. Some of these writers like Jorge Luis Borges are exclusively short story writers while others tried their hands in short story as well as novels. The economic underdevelopment and political unrest in the region could in no way affect its rich literary tradition. While discussing the causes behind the rich tradition of short story in Latin America Roberto Gonzalez Echevarria observes: "One important dimension of this long Latin American literary tradition is the quality and quantity of short stories it has produced. This can be explained in part by the convergence of narrative cycles from powerful and diverse cultural sources: the various native cultures (Aztec, Mayan, Incan, Guarani); the several African cultures (with the Yoruba prevailing); and the Iberian culture which includes the Portuguese, the Galician, and the Catalan, among others, as well as the entire European heritage reaching back, through the Middle Ages, to classical and biblical times and to the Indo-European sources of the Western narrative stock. But there are also more contingent reasons for the abundance of short story in Latin America. For instance, in a region fragmented into many countries sharing a language and a literature, the short story which travels easily, is a genre in which Latin American writers can come to know one another more rapidly"[2]. Echevarria also contends that of all the modern prose genres, the short story is both the most and the least literary—the most because the artistic short story is exact in matters of form and originality, and the least because the short story has a parallel oral tradition. He includes even gossips, anecdotes and jokes into the oral tradition of stories and gives the example of the story tellers of to-day's Venezuela who combine tradition and modern technology, selling cassettes of their performances. Case histories in psychoanalysis, anthropology and sociology have also contributed to the development of the genre. James G. Frazer's *The Golden Bough* (1890) and Sigmund Freud's *The Interpretation of Dreams* (1900) provoked the writers of story to collect materials from the innumerable incidents rendered in them. Karl Young pointed out the relation between the mythic stories and the subconscious where as Claude Levi-Strauss compared the deep structures of tales with those of language itself. To quote Echevarria, again, "The short story seems to be immune to time, to literary fashion, to progress, and to the diversity of cultures. Everyone, everywhere, has always told stories, although, although for purposes that differ according to the historical moment"[3].

Though the tradition of storytelling in the region started long before the 'New World' was exposed to the Europeans, thanks to Columbus, writing short story as a self conscious activity emerged as a result of the independence process during the first decades of the nineteenth century. When the areas marked as political subdivisions of the Spanish rule were declared independent nations, the elites of each region sought for their own literatures as marks of their independent nationhood and thus the national myth became the foundations of national literature. Though each nation was concerned with the progress of literature in its own area, political unrest in the entire land created a situation for mutual discussions. Intellectuals and writers from various Latin American countries met in Paris during nineteen thirties where they began to be aware of themselves and felt the necessity of a common platform to fight against the post independence evils. Most of them being exiled from their own countries, they could hardly gather in any Latin American city[4]. Moreover, Paris was the European hub of artistic and intellectual activities where short story as a genre was already established in the works of Maupassant, Flaubert and others and thus the Latin American writers were provided with an environment that helped them develop a new technique based on the essence of both the European and the Latin American traditions and earn worldwide reputation. The Peruvian writer of short story Richard Palma (1833-1919), was one of the first Latin American writers recognized abroad who focused on the quaint aspects of the colonial era as well as the contemporary quaintness of certain sections of Latin American reality. In his attempts to invent the past in his stories, one of the most compelling tasks confronting the Latin American intellectuals, Palma also highlights some inherent qualities of the native people---their honesty, integrity, self reliance and hard labor—which were inseparable from their religiosity and credulity. Take, for instance, two of his stories—'Fray Gomez's Scorpion' and 'Where and How the Devil Lost his Poncho.' In the former one, the writer starts with a saying "It is as valuable as Fray Gomez's scorpion" which was commonly used by the old women of his time while praising the beauty or value of a piece of jewelry. With the approach of a linguist, trying to find out the origin of the simile in the saying, the writer first brings out why Fray Gomez was accepted as a saint. He describes two incidents that were considered miraculous by the people and declares at the very outset that Fray Gomez performed miracles right and left, without even knowing that he was doing them, and as though against his will. It is also reported that Gomez was a born miracle-worker like the man who talked in prose without suspecting it. The first incident shows how the saint pronounced three blessings on a man whose brain was fractured and who lay stiff by the roadside, and the man got his feet as if nothing had happened. The writer offers two versions of what happened next. According to the first version, the mass assembled nearby shouted "A Miracle! A Miracle!," and in their enthusiasm they wanted to carry Fray Gomez in a triumphal procession. But Gomez started off at a run for his convent and shut himself in his room. According to the other version (provided in the Franciscan Chronicle), Fray Gomez, to escape from his admirers, rose in the air and flew to his convent. The author adds that he neither denies nor affirms the later version, and thus he sows the seeds of much talked about "magical realism" in Latin American literature. The other incident that took place on the same day was about Reverend Father San Francisco Solano who was suffering from a terrible headache and refused to any food. Gomez requested him to eat anything as he felt that it was necessary for his body to intake energy from some food. But San Francisco did not listen to him in spite of his repeated request. At last he said that he could eat a couple of smelts which was impossible to find during that season. But Gomez put his right hand into the left sleeve of his habit and pulled out two fresh smelts and those smelts cured San Francisco like a charm. The author comments that those miracles do not seem to him chaff and quotes from the lines inscribed on an oil painting depicting the two miracles he has described. The inscription offers a short bio sketch of Gomez who was born in1560, took the habit in 1580 and having worked as a nurse for forty years, displaying all virtues and celestial gifts, he died on second May, 1631. His life being a continuous miracle, he was ascribed sainthood. In a clever way the author gives evidence of Gomez's association with medical science offering the non-believers enough scope to interpret the 'miracles' in terms of medical science.

In the second part of the story Palma goes back to the task of narrating the origin of the saying. One day a ragged individual, crashed by poverty, called on Gomez in his cell-like room. Explaining how he badly needed money for promoting his business with which he could support his family, he asked for a loan of five hundred 'duros' only for six months. Moved by the poor man's faith in Gomez's capacity to arrange loan as well as in his own power to flourish with a trifle loan, Gomez blessed him. And running his eyes over the wall of his cell he saw a scorpion scrawling calmly along the window frame. He tore a page out of an old book and wrapped the scorpion, after picking it carefully, into the paper. Gomez gave the scorpion wrapped in paper to the man and told him that it was a jewel which could be pawned, and reminded him to return it after six month. The man's faith was so strong that he did not even try to have a look on what he received. He went directly to a pawnbroker who found in the packet a magnificent brooch in the shape of a scorpion and immediately offered the peddler the amount he wanted. The peddler did his business well and was able to return the brooch in time. When Gomez got it, he set it upon the windowsill blessing with the words, "Little creature of gold, go your way" and the scorpion began to scrawl. In this story of the saint's miraculous act of transforming an insect into an inanimate object Palma not only hints at the peddler's honesty and integrity but also points at the greed of the pawnbroker, the Spaniard, who hoped that after a time the peddler would come back for more money, and with the compound interest that would pile up, the peddler would have no other alternative but to give the jewel to him. The writer hints upon the greed of the colonial masters and their way of exploiting the poor natives with the use of the word 'Spaniard' and thus the hatred for the Spanish rule in Peru is expressed.

The story 'Where and How the Devil Lost His Poncho' begins rather in a dramatic way, with the words uttered by the narrator's friend Don Adeodato de la Mentirola who, the narrator informs, had taken up arms in the royalist cause with Colonel Sanjuanena and who still preferred the paternal rule of Fernando the Seventh to all the republic forms of government. That friend of the narrator kept all information about Bolivar's philandering with the ladies of Lima and also about the old scandals. The story of the Devil's losing his poncho when he came to Ica in the guise of Jesus is presented in the version of the narrator's friend and apparently, the narrator is relieved of giving explanations in regard to the happenings in the story. However, the narrator makes it clear that there is no record of the arrival of Jesus and his disciples in the region, and nor was there a thing like the telegraph or a steamboat or a printing press as described in the story. He therefore asks the readers to overlook these and other anachronisms and enjoy. In this story also, which is narrated as a joke, simplicity of the local people and their inherent love for peace is suggested. According to the story, Lord Jesus accompanied by His disciples came to Ica while travelling all over the world, healing the diseased. They liked the peaceful place so much and were treated with so much hospitality that they continued to stay there for some days. But one day Jesus received a telegram urging Him to return to Jerusalem at once to keep the Samaritan woman from pulling out Mary Magdalene's hair, and He decided to leave the place without the knowledge of a soul. The villagers missed Him and His disciples next morning and felt sorry. Having read in the newspaper the details of celebration and banquets bestowed on Jesus, Devil grew jealous and planned to visit Ica in the guise of Christ. The people of Ica, gullible as they were, received Devil and the disciples thinking that the Master had come back and Devil began to enjoy the luxurious treatment. But soon the peace of the region was gone: the lawyers and notaries got together to drum up trade; the doctors and druggists went into cahoots to raise the price of medicine; the mothers-in-law decided to scratch out their sons-in-law's eyes; the wives began to whine and beg for jewelry and velvet dresses; and the town council declared that they would have to tax people ten cents for each sneeze. After this funny yet realistic description of the evils caused by the Devil's presence, the story teller declares that there was anarchy with all its horrors, people divided into two groups of rowdies, attacking each other. The story ends with an innocent bride's appeal to the Devil, supposed to be Christ Himself, to make an end of the anarchy; no sooner did the Devil saw the girl's fingers forming the sign of cross, than he tried to rush off like a dog with a firecracker tied to its tail; and as the girl had held the corner of his dress (poncho) tightly, the Devil had to slip his head through the opening of the poncho, leaving it in the bride's hand. It is said that the Satan often comes to Ica in search of his lost poncho. This funny story may or may not be interpreted as a symbolic one. But its worth as a precursor of magic realism in which fact and fantasy co-exist cannot be denied. Palma shows the way how realistic description can be blended with miracles and mysteries.

In contemporary Latin America, Jorge Luis Borges is the leading short story writer who is also recognized as one of the best in the world and he had immense influence on Gabriel Garcia Marquez in his formation period. He openly expressed his disgust for novel, which he found amorphous and tedious. In a famous prologue to Adolfo Bioy Casares's *La invencion de Morel* (1940), Borges said that the lengthy work of Proust was as boring as life and also opposed the psychological novel. In preface to the volume *A Universal History of Iniquity* (1935), he said about his own writing, "Certain techniques are overused: mismatched lists, abrupt transitions, and the reduction of a person's entire life to two or three scenes. The stories are not, nor are they attempted to be, psychological." The novelty that Borges brought in his stories is suggested in this remark. He opposed the trend of realistic novel, particularly the novels written in different regions of Latin America with an aim to expose social ills through detailed descriptions of the rural scenario. For him those 'realistic social novels' were nothing but opportunistic political program. He chose to maintain absolute artificiality of fiction. As it was a common practice in his time to use colloquial terms and slangs in the dialogue of the lower class people, he did just the opposite and offered explanation for what he did. About the story 'Man on Pink Corner' he wrote in the preface to the 1954 edition of the volume *A Universal History of Iniquity,* "In that text, which is written in the accents of the toughs and petty criminals of the Buenos Aires underworld, I have interpolated a number of 'cultured' words—entrails, conversion etc. I did this because the tough, the knife fighters, the thug, the type that Buenos Aires calls the 'compadre' or 'compradito' aspires to refinement or because 'compadres' are individuals and don't always talk like the Compadre, which is a platonic ideal." In many of his stories a vexing philosophical problem is raised openly and that too in an apparently light context like that of a detective story.

Though Borges did not like to be associated with what came in vogue by the name of 'magic realism'[5], his preoccupation with vast themes involving the very creation of the universe and the origin of mankind—themes opposed to that of the social realists who harp on the hardships of mediocre heroes—brings him close to such writers as Alejo Carpentier, famous for bringing 'magic' in Latin American fiction. Borges's 'Tlon, Uqbar, Orbis Tertius' which is the account of the completely artificial construction of a region, might have inspired Marquez to create Macondo, the backdrop of some of his stories and of the celebrated novel *One Hundred Years of Solitude*. A detailed analysis of a story written by Borges may be helpful in this discussion. Take, for example, the story 'The Garden of Forking Paths' which exhibits the main characteristics of Borges's writing such as his use of metaphysical riddles in fiction, raising questions on reality as well as the validity of art and the use of the narrative method of a detective story. The story starts with an incident during the First World War recorded in history. It is about the mystery of postponing a planned offensive by thirteen British divisions against the German line at Serre-Montauban. It was scheduled for July 24, but was postponed till 29th, presumably for torrential rain which had in fact no significance. This news is followed by a copy of the report made by one Dr. Yu Tsun, a British spy, and the first two pages of the report were missing. The story keeps suspense till the end and the concluding lines seek to clarify why after such a long and terrifying journey Yu Tsun killed the old sinologist Albert. He desperately wanted to highlight the name of the city Albert, the name of the exact site of the new British artillery park on the Ancre, to his boss as he overheard Captain Richard Madden uttering the name of the city as their target. He had no other course open to him than to kill someone of that name, he said, and he was sure that the news of the murder having been published in big newspapers, his purpose of sending the name was served. Within the plot of this story there are several reflections on time: Yu Tsun thinks, "all things happen, happen to one, precisely now. Century follows century, and things happen only in the present"; again, "I thought of a maze of mazes, of a sinuous, ever growing maze which would take in both past and future and would somehow involve the stars." Stephen Albert says to Yu Tsun about Ts'ui Pen's book, *The Garden of Forking Paths*: "*The Garden of Forking Paths* is an enormous guessing game, or parable, in which the subject is time. The rules of the game forbid the use of the word itself. . . . I have translated the whole work. I can state categorically that not once has the word time been used in the whole book. The explanation is obvious. *The Garden of Forking Paths* is a picture, incomplete yet not false, of the universe such as Ts'ui Pen conceived it to be. Differing from Newton and Schopenhauer, your ancestor did not think of time as absolute and uniform. He believed an infinite series of times, in a dizzily growing, ever spreading network of diverging, converging and parallel times. This web of time—the strands of which approach one another, bifurcate, intersect or ignore each other through the centuries–embraces every possibility." The story also includes hallucinations and day-dreaming, if not miracles. While conversing with Albert the narrator felt around him something intangible pullulating. He also has the sensation that the dew damp garden surrounding the house was infinitely saturated with invisible people. However, the nightmare disappeared soon. With all this there is violence and terror. Borges's blending of diverse materials in his fiction must have inspired Marquez to bring together materials as diverse as love and violence in his fictional writings.

Marquez's early stories were written in modernist mode, concentrating on the protagonist's self-analysis, awareness of split personality, often a fear of death and they are full of images of death and also of dullness, dampness, bad smell and nausea. The first collection of his stories *Eyes of a Blue Dog* contains such stories, exhibiting his experiments with narrative technique and form of fiction. His first published story 'The Third Resignation' included in this volume is based on an absurd situation: the protagonist, a sickly young man of twenty five, who had been lying in coffin since he was seven when he died for the first time, finally resigns to death. After his first death he continued to grow physically, though there was no other sign of life in his body and his coffin had to be changed. After his second death his body ceased to grow further and he did not even need to breath; he became happy for this. Then he was overpowered with a sudden fear that he would be buried alive, for he could deduce logically that he could not be dead because he had an exact awareness of everything. Finally he consoles himself with the thought that if he would not be buried at that time the smell that had started coming out of his coffin would be so strong that his relatives and neighbors would flee in fright, holding a handkerchief to their mouths. Hence he heard the last prayer with resignation He removed from his mind all possibilities of being alive and "he is so resigned to dying now that he might well die from resignation" (10). The story reminds one of Kafka, Camus and their contemporaries in its delineation of morbid situations, almost clinical self analysis and animal imagery. The very first lines of the story may be quoted as an example of bringing a morbid situation:

> There was that noise again. That cold, cutting, vertical noise that he knew so well now; it was spinning around inside his empty head, dull and biting. A beehive had risen up inside the four walls of his scull. . . . Something had become unadapted in his human material structure, something that had functioned normally 'at other times' and now was hammering at his head from within with dry and hard blows . . . and it made him remember all the bitter sensations of life. . . . He would have liked to catch the noise that was piercing the moment with its sharp diamond point between the palms of his sensitive hands. The figure of a domestic cat made his muscles contract when he imagined it chasing through the tormented corners of his hot fever-torn head. Now he would catch it. No. The noise had slippery fur, almost untouchable.[1]

The description of the protagonist's deaths also reveals his capacity for self analysis. After his first death when he found himself "untouchable, unspatial, nonexistent" inside the coffin, he acknowledged him to be lethargic and passive. He felt dull and listless. He knew that if he would try to get up he could do it easily, at least spiritually. But he was not ready to take the trouble and thought it better to let himself die. After his second death he was happy because his body rested peacefully with no discomfort and he need not take the trouble of breathing even. The fear that overpowered him was due to his anticipation of losing comfort. One is reminded of J. Alfred Prufrock's preference for cozy comfort to the trouble of disturbing the world with overwhelming question (T.S. Eliot). A typical modernist anxiety for losing one's unity may also be discerned in the protagonist's reflections: "One day, however, he will feel his armor fall apart. . .He will feel that he doesn't have any definitive, exact form. . .that he has lost his unity" (7). The images used in the story are also typically modernist.

'The Other Side of Death' is another story written on the model of Kafka, creating an atmosphere of terror, rendering morbid self-analysis and images. In this story, the use of the third person narrator and the first person narrator at the same time creates confusion. The protagonist's twin brother, who is killed, is ultimately rendered as his other self, opening up multiple possibilities in regard to the condition of the brother's dead body, there being one that the buried brother may remain incorruptible while the living brother would be rotten. The protagonist's review of the previous moments in his mind is proof of his capacity of self analysis including the analysis of his dream as well as his body and environment in a queer way:

> It was his absurd irrational dream, of course, but there was no reason for it to have caused that restless awakening. . . He felt that he had fallen on the soft and thick cushion while his body, light and weightless, had been run through by a sweet feeling of beatitude and fatigue and was losing consciousness of its own material structure, that heavy, earthy substance that defined it, placing it in an unmistakable and exact spot on the zoological scale and bearing a whole sum of systems, geometrically defined organs that lifted him up to the arbitrary hierarchy of rational animals. . .as if the whole organism had turned into one single, large, total organism, and he the man—had abandoned his moral roots so as to penetrate other, deeper and firmer, roots: the eternal roots of an integral and definitive dream. Outside, from the other side of the world, he could hear the cricket's song growing weaker until it disappeared from his senses, which had turned inward, submerging him in a new and uncomplicated notion of time and space, erasing

> the presence of that material world, physical and painful, full of insects and acrid smells of violets and formaldehyde (12-13).

The protagonist's abandoning moral roots for the eternal roots of an 'integral and definitive dream' puts forward the philosophical discourse on reality in a different way, paving the path for 'magical' reality. Borges's speculation on time may also be noted in the concept of 'uncomplicated' time and space. The speaker's repeated confusion in demarcating reality from dream, the idea of his twin brother's corpse firmly "stuck in the whole center of his life," the use of simile such as "death began to flow through his bones like a river of ashes," the concept of 'another body' sunken with him in the liquid night of the maternal womb and climbing up with him through the branches of an ancient genealogy—the blood of his four pairs of grandparents and that from the beginning of the world—and the protagonist's feeling that the drops from the sky would "fill the room in the space of an hour or in thousand years" and that it dropped from "the other world in the mistaken and absurd world of rational creatures" reveal Marquez's desperate attempt to arrive at a new mode of narration, based on but different from the modes used by his predecessors.

In stories like 'Iva is Inside her Cat' the author tries to deal with problems of daily life in an atmosphere of mystery, keeping aside the repeated philosophical reflections on time or on dream and reality. In this story, a beautiful woman's problems—she was tired of being the center of attention, of being under siege from men's long looks during day time and during sleepless nights she craved for being an ordinary woman—are rendered almost following the technique used by Kafka. The woman feels in her despair that the insects which seem to be "terrible creatures" to her, were part of her own organism and that they might come from her father who "had fed them painfully during his nights of desperate solitude" or maybe they had poured into her arteries "through the cord that linked her to her mother ever since the beginning of the world." She cursed her ancestors for her beauty which was the cause of her insomnia and during day time she remembered how with her big and round eyes, open and frightened, she bore the weight of the darkness that "fell upon her temples like molten lead." She was then haunted by her childhood memory—of the drowned 'boy' who had been buried in their courtyard under the orange tree and who, she was afraid, would ask her defend him from other insects or would ask her let him sleep beside her as he did when he was alive. She thought of incarnating herself in a cat but was afraid that as a cat one day she would have in her palate, in her throat, in all her quadruped organism, the irrevocable desire to eat a mouse and then she would no longer feel any desire to eat an orange that she so desired now. Though she overpowered her fear and wanted to be an intelligent cat, the cat was found nowhere in the house and a strong smell of arsenic beat on her nostrils. Only then, as says the concluding sentence, she understood that "three thousand years had passed since the day she had had a desire to eat the first orange." The mystery in the ending suggests Marquez's search for a new narrative technique other than that of Kafka. In the story 'Eyes of a Blue Dog,' dream and reality are given a common space in the love of a man and a woman who are united in their dreams and have the only clue to find each other during day time in the phrase "eyes of a blue dog." The woman searched for the man of her dream loudly uttering the words "eyes of a blue dog" on the street, and also writing those words on every possible places that she found, with the hope that the man of her dream would recognize the words and come to her. For, none of them could recognize the other from the face or the overall appearance. The narrator of the story, who is also the male character in it, says about the woman of his dream, "Her life had been dedicated to finding me in reality, through the identifying phrase: 'Eyes of a Blue Dog'" (45). The description of their union when they recognize each other after the man said to her 'eyes of a blue dog,' first appears to have happened in reality, but at the end of the story it is clear that this union too, is performed in dream and hardly has any connection to reality. The story ends with the man's declaration that he must recognize her when he would find some woman on the street writing "eyes of a blue dog" and the woman's sad reply that he would remember nothing as he was the only man who forgets everything of what he dreamed when he wakes up.

The story 'Monologue of Isabel Watching It Rain in Macondo' is remarkable as neither the protagonist nor the place is unnamed and moreover, the protagonist is a woman. Here Marquez uses the backdrop of Macondo, a fictional reconstruction of the Caribbean town Aracataca, where he was born and this backdrop has been used in some of his most significant writings. The theme is torrential rain that affects the pregnant protagonist in such a way that she loses all sense of time. Typical features of a tropical, coastal land—the unbearable heat and humidity of the hot seasons and the seasons of incessant rains and strong winds—are rendered to present a true picture of the land. Isabel remembers the months of heat: "those long and awesome siestas in which we dropped down to die under the weight of the hour, our clothes sticking to our bodies, hearing outside the insistent and dull buzzing of the hour that never passed"(83). Though the first arrival of rain after heat is most welcome, the continuous rainfall that changes overnight the harsh gray earth of May into a dark sticky substance like a cheap soap, works on one's nerves, keeping everybody confined at home and developing the sense that it will never clear. In her monologue Isabel records her feelings during the incessant rain: "We were paralyzed, drugged by the rain, given over to the collapse of nature with a peaceful and resigned attitude" (85); a terrible feeling of emptiness overpowered her as she found that the water was up to her ankles and the entire house was flooded; penetrating smell of decomposing bodies disturbed her though her husband said that it was the imagination of a pregnant woman. Side by side with such picture of mundane reality, there are recorded experiences of mystery as when Isabel heard her husband Martin sitting beside her complained that the weather bored him. Isabel replied him immediately and turned to look at him but found the empty chair. The end of the story, again, is full of mystery as it describes Isabel's feelings after the weather became normal. After a sleep of many hours when she got up, she was struck by the violent silence of the house. Suddenly she felt her heart turned into stone and thought she was dead. Only after she heard Martin's unpleasant voice, she realized that it had cleared and the silence stretched out all around was a mysterious and deep beatitude, "a perfect state which must have been very much like death." Something in the air revealed the presence of an invisible person who was smiling in the darkness. And Isabel felt that she would not be surprised if someone would call her to go to last Sunday's mass when the rain started. Thus for Isabel the entire period of torrential rain might just be her dream. The violence of previous stories is here replaced by the protagonist's mysterious feelings, suggesting Marquez's ongoing search for a suitable style of fiction writing.

The second volume of Marquez's collected stories *Big Mama's Funeral* contains stories which are markedly different from the stories included in the previous collection. His zeal for revealing the political corruption—oppression inflicted on the poor and the people of the opposition—compelled him to change the mode of narration, adding sharp irony and black humor to the exaggerated version of real events. Take, for example, the short story, 'One of These Days.' In this story, Aurelio Escovar, a dentist without a degree, more concerned with the weather than with his practice, is seen arranging his instruments in order of size with much concentration. He is disturbed when his eleven year old son announces the presence of the mayor at his door for pulling his tooth. The dentist asks his son to report to the mayor that he was not there. The son goes to the waiting room and shouts from there that the mayor can hear his voice and is ready to shoot him if he does not appear. Without hurrying and maintaining an extremely tranquil movement, the dentist asks the boy to call the mayor and also gets his revolver ready. The mayor is portrayed as a funny figure as he appears at the door. The left side of his face is clean shaved, while the other side, swollen and visibly in pain, has a five-day-old beard. A similar situation is found in *In Evil Hour* where the dialogue is little bit changed. The mayor and the dentist exchange wishes however, instead of using revolver. Sitting on the chair meant for patients the mayor leans his head on the headrest of the chair and feels better. After inspecting the infected tooth the dentist declares that the tooth has to be pulled without anesthesia. As the mayor wants to know the cause, the dentist says it is because he has an abscess. The details of the operation are given along with the picture of the mayor's pain as he seizes the arm of the chair, braces his feet with all his strength and feels an icy void in his kidneys without making a sound. But the conversation that follows is hardly expected from a dentist and his patient. The dentist says that the mayor has to pay for twenty dead men. He also asks the Mayor if the bill will be sent to him or to the town and the mayor replies that there is no difference. It becomes clear that the mayor, a representative of the ruling dictator staying afar, holds supreme power in the town and all his expenses are met by the government. It is likely that the dentist asks the question only to remind him that the town pays for his personal expenses and instead he is working against the men of the town. It has already been suggested that he is the man behind the assassination of twenty men belonging to the opposing party (Liberal Party) and the dentist, an activist of the Liberal Party, takes revenge as he gets the opportunity of taunting him and inflicting physical torture on him without using anesthesia. In a similar situation in the novel *In Evil Hour* the dentist says in reply to the mayor's grumbling that they never use anesthesia while killing people. A slice of the picture of the Civil War in Colombia is presented in the story.

The stories like 'There are no Thieves in This Town' and 'Balthazar's Marvelous Afternoon' are simple realistic stories which hardly have anything common either with fantasy or with Kafka's model. These stories concentrate on the psychology of simple people who have their own standard of right and wrong and who still retain humanistic feelings in the midst of a mechanized society. 'There are no Thieves in the Town' starts with suspense as the protagonist Damaso's pregnant wife Ana, seventeen years older than him, was waiting for him in their bed till the crack of dawn when Damasco entered his room carrying a bundle of red cloth. Ana fixed her frightened eyes on the bundle and began to tremble, pressing her lips together. At last it is found that the bundle contained three billiard balls which had been used in the club for playing billiard. It also comes out that Damaso had stolen those balls as there was nothing else. Ana expressed her concern for him, urging that he must have remembered that she was there, unable to sleep, apprehending that he would be brought home dead. As Ana also expressed her dissatisfaction over the amount of the stolen material, Damaso said that there was only twenty five cents in the drawer. He told her the details of his adventure and it appears that the couple had good understanding among themselves. Ana assured him that he need not bother about money, risking his life, as long as she was continuing her laundry work. She also gathered news about the theft in the club house from other people and listened to the details of the same event from several persons. Initially it was learnt that the thief must have been a stranger, as there was no thief in the town. Ana accused Damaso of lying, as everybody was talking that two hundred pesos was stolen. Damaso replied that that was an utter lie and told with much confidence that there was only twenty five cents. Ana believed in what he said and when he was going out after three hours of getting dressed, she gave him a peso for pocket money. As he was enjoying himself in the roofless theatre, he was alarmed with the shout "thief! Thief!" and for a moment felt himself discovered. But soon his fear was gone as he saw a gigantic Negro, rolled between the rows of chairs and chased by two policemen who struck at his kidneys until they managed to grab him from behind. Damaso became restless at heart and coming back at home buried the billiard balls under the bed. He did not much respond to Ana when she informed him of the arrest of a Negro for theft. She understood from his reaction that he had gone to the movie and had witnessed the arrest. Though there was hardly any threat of life for him, the couple could not but think about the aftermath of the theft. As the owner of the club could not purchase new billiard balls because of their rising cost, the people in the town were denied the opportunity of playing billiard and seeing the game for enjoyment. There was also rumor that the club might be shut down. Frustrated by the result of his own action, Damaso wanted to start a business in billiard balls outside the town and wanted some loan from Ana. But Ana was fully aware of his lack of tricks needed very much in business and she refused to give him money for business. Thereon Damaso got angry and left his home. As there was hardly any taboo on sex in Colombia, Damaso spent two days with another woman, supposed to be prostitute, who told him that the Negro had not stolen as he was staying with a woman in the locality by that time. With this news, Damaso's uneasiness returned as he was now afraid that in case that woman would confess that the Negro had been with her by the time of theft, a fresh search to find the thief out was likely to start again. Moreover, there was always the biting conscience for being responsible for the Negro's plight. Disturbed with these thoughts he came back again to his home to find his wife Ana as calmly waiting for him as before. And surprisingly, both of them started thinking about returning the billiard balls to their original place so that the gesture could enable the people of the town to enjoy themselves in the club, though in no way the sufferings of the Negro could be relieved. The story ends with Damaso's being caught red handed while returning the billiard balls in a moonlit night. The owner of the club, an unsympathetic, greedy and cruel fellow, declared that he would take the story to the mayor and he was determined to bring false charges of stealing two hundred pesos against Damaso, calling him a fool. In this story Marquez offers a true picture of a so- called fool and a clever man in society and ironically shows—the irony is evident in the title of the story—that a clever man who cheats others, bringing false accusation on them, is never exposed but a man having conscience and good will may be falsely accused as a thief only if he is simple enough and hardly unaware of the art of duplicity, The story at once reminds one of a story by Tolstoy, though the moral tone is missing. A similar story is 'Balthazar's Marvelous Afternoon' in which Marquez brings out an artisan's simple joy in creating a work of art set against the greed and lack of artistic sense of the affluent. Balthazar, the protagonist in the story is however a poor carpenter who is engaged in making cages for birds, neglecting the work of his carpenter's shop. That afternoon, having finished his cage when he hung it under the eave, many people gathered there who appreciated the cage as the most beautiful one in the world. The news was spread around the town and an old physician of the town Dr. Octavio Giraldo, happy with life but tired of his profession and already having two cages with canaries liked by his invalid wife, thought about purchasing Balthazar's cage. That distinguished person went to the carpenter's home to inspect the cage and was simply moved as he found the cage much more beautiful than any he had ever dreamed of for his wife. Balthazar blushed and thanked him. But when he wanted to purchase it, Balthazar told that the cage could not be sold as it had been ordered and it belonged to the son of

Mr. Chepe Montiel. The doctor wanted to know if Chepe Montiel or his son gave him the design. After Balthazar replied in the negative, the doctor said that in that case he was free to sell it and wanted to know how much Montiel would pay for the cage. Balthazar did not reply first and looked at his wife who replied that it was sixty pesos. The doctor took leave with the words that Montiel was a rich person. Marquez's rather ironic description of the rich man may be quoted in this context. "In truth, Jose Montiel was not as rich as he seemed, but he would have been capable of doing anything to become so. A few blocks from there, in a house crammed with equipment, where no one had ever smelled a smell that couldn't be sold, he remained indifferent to the news of the cage. His wife tortured with the obsession of death, closed the doors and windows after lunch and lay for two hours with her eyes opened to the shadow of the room, while, where Jose Monitel took his siesta"(130). Such a man can hardly be expected as a bier of a cage, that too at the price of fifty pesos. Exactly that happened. Not only that. Montiel also scolded and beat his son for giving the order of a cage without taking his consent. Balthazar was humiliated for taking order from a minor and was given back the cage. "The child had remained motionless, without blinking, until Balthazar looked at him uncertainly with the cage in his hand. Then he emitted a guttural sound, like a dog's growl, and threw himself on the floor screaming" (132). But Montiel remained unmoved at this show and even forbade his wife to console the child and advised her to let the boy break his head on the floor and then apply salt and lemon on his scar. Balthazar observed the child as he would have observed the death throes of a rabid animal. Balthazar approached the child smiling and held the cage out to him. The child jumped up, embraced the cage and stood looking at Balthazar not knowing what to tell him. Montiel told Balthazar that he was already asked to leave the place with his cage. But Balthazar replied that he had made it for the child and he now gave him as a gift. Montiel yet started shouting asking him to take the cage back and forbidding all to order for anything in his absence. As Balthazar came out of Montiel's home without paying heed to what he was saying, he met his friends who had accompanied him there. Surprised, his friends wanted to know if he really got fifty pesos, and Balthazar replied that he received sixty. His friends then demanded a treat and all of them started drinking bear, Balthazar got drunk soon and then delivered a lecture on a fabulous project of making a million cages and selling them at sixty pesos each to all the rich men in the town before they die. His wife received the news that he was in the pull hall buying beer for everybody, but she did not believe it as he was not in the habit of drinking outside. Yet for the first time in his life Balthazar lay "spread-eagled in the street"; he left his watch in pawn for buying beer and his shoes were taken off as he lay unconscious. In this story Marquez openly criticizes the rich men's way of life—their excessive attachment to matter and their lack of fine sensibilities including the ability to enjoy a work of art that alone gives meaning to one's existence. Such rich persons are rendered as sick—they are destined to be physically sick for their unnecessary tensions regarding material loss in addition to their spiritual sickness. Written in simple realistic mode these stories have a universal appeal.

'Big Mama's Funeral' has almost all the qualities in it for which Marquez has been appreciated all over the world: an urgency to record the happenings (often political) that are usually erased from official records, exaggerated version of persons and incidents mainly for satire, humor mixed with satire, a peculiar blending of reality and fantasy and above all, a narrative mode that takes the reader into confidence, delineating fantastic events as if they are being witnessed by the author. Big Mama is rendered as the last in the line of dictators who had ruled the kingdom of Macondo for two hundred years. Having suffered for a period of fourteen weeks Big Mama breathed her last at the age of ninety two, and it was unexpected for all as it had not occurred to anyone that Big Mama was mortal. The narrator intends to give details of her dying hours as well as her life and wealth, lest some vital parts of her life and work are erased by the historians. She died a virgin and childless as she had rejected the most passionate suitors until she was fifty. No one could be indifferent to this death, as all were affected by it. To describe her dominance over others the author uses the method of exaggeration that is full of humor: "Big Mama had been Macondo's center of gravity, as had her brothers, her parents, and the parents of her parents in the past, in a dominance which covered two centuries. The town was founded on her surname. No one knew the origin, or the limits of the real value of her estate, but everyone was used to believing that Big Mama was the owner of the waters, running and still, of rain and drought, and of the district's roads, telegraph poles, leap years and heat waves, and that she had furthermore a hereditary right over life and property" (172). Sharp political satire is evident in the rhetorical remarks used in the author's proposal of covering a report on Big Mama's death:

> Now that the nation, which was shaken to its vitals, has recovered its balance now that the bagpipers of San Jacinto, the smugglers of Guajira, the rice planters of Sinu, the prostitutes of Caucamayal, the wizards of Sierpe, and the banana workers of Aracataca have folded up their tents to recover from the exhausting vigil and have regained their serenity, and the President of the Republic and his Ministers and those who represented the public and super-natural powers on the most magnificent funeral occasion recorded in the annuls of history have regained control of their estates; now that the Holy Pontiff has risen up to Heaven in body and soul; and now that it is impossible to walk around in Macondo because of the empty bottles, the cans and rags and excrement that the crowd which came to the burial left behind; now is the time to lean a stool against the front door and relate from the beginning the details of

> this national commotion, before the historians have chance to get at it (170).

Big Mama's attachment to her wealth even at the time of her death is also sarcastically revealed in the lines that describe how she, having put the affairs of her soul in order with the help of Father Anthony Isabel, needed to put her worldly affairs in order with her nine nieces and nephews, her sole heirs, who were standing around her bed. She called her nieces 'Highway Robbers' as they circled around the dying lady, looking greedily at her hands "bejeweled with precious stones." Big Mama's luxurious birthday celebration, her intention to keep up the family wealth under her control through arrangement of marriages among near relatives, thereby turning procreation into a vicious circle, her collection of rents from three hundred and fifty two tenant farmers—all are rendered in an inimitable style, full of subtle irony and satire. This story is thus a landmark with its inclusion of the fictitious backdrop of Macondo, blending of stark reality and exaggerated version verging on fantasy, sharp satire on patriarchal rule and such others.

The third volume of Marquez's stories *The Incredible and Sad Tale of Innocent Irendira and Her Heartless Grandmother,* was translated by Gregory Rabassa, The author's capacity to render marvelous things as possible and probable is perhaps best exemplified in his story, 'A Very Old Man with Enormous Wings' included in this volume. The story has the look of a fairy tale in a realistic setting: on the third day of a continuous rainfall in a coastal town, Pelayo found in the back of his courtyard an old man, lying face down in the mud, who, in spite of his tremendous efforts, couldn't get up, impeded by his enormous wings. "Frightened by the nightmare," Pelayo called his wife Elisenda and both of them looked at the creature so long and so closely that they soon "overcame their surprise and in the end found him familiar." They even dared to speak to him and he answered in an incomprehensible dialect with a strong sailor's voice. So they concluded that he was a lonely castaway from some foreign ship wrecked by the storm. But when their neighbor identified him as an angel who must have come there to cure their ailing newborn, the couple rescued the creature and gave him a shelter in their chicken coop. The baby was cured soon and the couple felt magnanimous; they decided to put the creature on a raft with fresh water and provisions for three days and leave him to his fate on the high seas. But they found the whole neighborhood in front of the chicken coop having fun with the creature. The strange news also drew Father Gonzaga of the nearest church who, unable to decide whether the creature with a human look could be given the dignity of an angel only because of his wings, that too strewn with parasites, promised to write a letter to his bishop to decide the matter. No letter came from the bishop however, but the number of visitors rapidly increased and Elisenda got the idea of fencing in the yard and charging five cents admission to see the "angel." In less than a week the couple crammed their rooms with money and the flow of money continued till there arrived the travelling show of a woman who had been changed into a spider for having disobeyed her parents. Finally, when the creature ceased to draw visitors who now preferred the woman changed into a spider, the creature was one day seen capable of flying, passing over the last houses of the town, holding himself up in some way with the risky flapping of a senile vulture. The story with the flatness of its plot is as impersonal as a newspaper clipping, reporting odd events in detail, and the narrator's intention is, clearly, not the revelation of the creature's identity but an exposure of the human psyche. The couple in the story had little interest in anything but money and their inhuman behavior is explicit in their callous treatment of the creature, whose presence, according to their neighbor, cured their ailing baby. It is a suffocating situation of loveless relationships based on material gain. The cruelty of the mass as revealed in their dealings with the creature and their interest in magic for their selfish benefit are sketched with some bold strokes that reveal the hollowness of modern civilization. Though set in a coastal town in Colombia, the story with its bizarre incidents reveals true human nature. While in 'Metamorphosis' Kafka reinvented fable by placing it in the modern quotidian world, Marquez reset fairy tale in the landscape of the third world in his story 'A Very Old Man with Enormous Wings.' The bureaucratic procedure in Kafka's story is replaced with the common man's interest in magic for personal benefit in Marquez's story and both the stories introduce spiritual issues in their respective ways. But it is the distracting and the disorienting effect of Marquez's story that differentiates his art from that of his predecessor.

'The Incredible and Sad Tale of Innocent Erendira and Her Heartless Grandmother' is perhaps the most horrifying of all the stories of Marquez. Almost a novella in size, it is a description of the torture inflicted on a fourteen year old orphan girl—the incredible account of making money by using the girl as a whore who is compelled to receive unaccountable customers each day—by her grandmother who is rendered as the most cruel dictator, heartless and money minded. It needs indeed a very powerful imagination to create such a demonic figure. She is introduced physically in the beginning of the story as a handsome white whale taking her bath in a huge marble tub with water in which purifying herbs and aromatic leaves had been boiled, her metal-colored hair and powerful shoulders, mercilessly tattooed as to put sailors to shame. Her granddaughter, languid, soft-boned and too meek for her age, was engaged in bathing her with a parsimony that had something like sacred rigor about it. Erendira is burdened with innumerable household chores besides bathing and dressing her grandmother who was so fast that she could walk only by leaning on her granddaughter's shoulder. She needed two hours to get her grandmother ready after bath: she untangled her hair strand by strand, perfumed and combed it, put an equatorially flowered dress on her, put talcum powder on her face, bright lipstick on her mouth, rouge on her cheeks, mask on her eyelids, polish on her nails and then led her to an artificial garden with suffocating flowers where she was seated on a large chair having the pedigree of a throne. The house was in the heart of the desert where, according to the local Indians, the old woman's husband Amadis transplanted his beautiful wife, having rescued her from a house of prostitution in the Antilles. He died of melancholy fever and his son, also called Amadises, was riddled with bullets in a fight over a woman and bodies of both were buried in the courtyard. After their death the servant girls were dismissed and Irendira had to do everything from to midnight. One night out of tiredness she forgot to put out the candle before going to bed and it caught fire, demolishing everything. In Marquez's arresting style of description, "the wind of her misfortune came into the bedroom like a pack of hounds and knocked the candle over against the curtain" (248). Next morning the grandmother declared that Irendira would have to pay her back for the mishap and it was through selling her body. The price of her virginity was decided to be two hundred and twenty pesos and some provisions. And after that the grandmother left no stone unturned to sell her body. She started moving around, carrying with the help of the Indian laborers tents and other household materials along with the remnants of the bodies of Amadises in a trunk. In different places of the desert area tent was set for business and there were long queues in front of Irendira's tent. The grandmother sitting in front of the tent took the fixed money from each and let them enter one after another. All the appeals of Erndira to her grandmother were unheeded and she had to undergo the agony of repeated rapes every day. Once she was rescued by some missionaries in a church which was devoted to sheltering prostitutes and gets them married in possible cases. When the grandmother failed to get Irendira back from the clutches of the church, she devised a plan. She arranged a boy for twenty pesos who would tell the missionary that he was willing to marry Irendira and after the marriage he was to give her back to the old woman. The plan work and the business were going on as usual. Among the customers, one boy named Ulises, the son of a smuggler, fell in love with Irendira and both of them even planned to escape. But the plan was foiled and henceforth the poor girl's leg was tied to a dog chain. The story ends with Ulises's coming back to Irendira, his killing the old woman with much effort on Irendira's request and Irendira's running away with the gold vest without looking at Ulises. This melodramatic story weighs on one's nerves and it is difficult for any reader to erase the images from the mind. The story contains some of the characteristics of a Marquez story such as exaggeration, presentation of improbable incidents and forceful narration. Marquez's faith in the existence of true love that lies beyond the barriers of time and space is also revealed here. An atmosphere of fantasy is created trough some incidents: after Ulises fell in love with Irendira, the glasses he touched changed colors; the blood coming out of the grandmother's body was shiny and blue; in the end Erendira kept on running with the gold vest beyond the arid winds and the never-ending sunsets and she was never heard of again nor was the slightest trace of her misfortune ever found.

The last collection of Marquez's stories *Strange Pilgrims* (Spanish *Doce cuentos peregrines*) was published in 1993, though the stories were written during the seventies and eighties. The stories were translated into English by Edith Grossman. It is a collection of twelve stories, all written on experiences of dislocation and strangeness in exile. In 'Bon Voyage Mr. President' an overthrown Latin American President, unnamed as usual, is exiled to Martinique at the age of seventy three where he lives as a common man, having lost all his wealth and also his relatives. Suffering not only from solitude but also from an acute pain in his lower body—his ribs, lower abdomen and groin—he becomes restless and goes to Geneva for diagnosis and treatment. After extensive medical testing it is reported that the problem resides in his spine and he is recommended an operation, at the risk of his life. The man who had enjoyed the most luxurious life possible on earth is now unable to collect the amount required for his operation. By this time he meets a common man there who has come from the President's own country. That man Homero Rey, an ambulance driver at the hospital, schemes to sell an insurance plan and financial package to the President, having no idea that he could be reduced to the position of a poor man who has to sell the ornaments of his deceased wife to meet the expenses of his medical treatment. Homero and his wife Lazara grew fond of the president, providing him with financial assistance as well as care needed during convalescence. The President goes back to Martinique, but finds that he is not relieved of the pain in his lower body which however has not aggravated. He considers going back to his country as the head of a reform group. The story 'The Saint' centers on a common man Margarito, who is originally from the small Andean village of Tolima in Colombia and who has gone to Rome in order to start the process of gaining the status of sainthood for her deceased daughter. The narrator of the story meets him in Rome at the 'pensione' where both of them stayed for some time. The narrator learns that the man had lost his wife shortly after the birth of their only daughter who also died at the age of seven. Eleven years after the death of the girl the villagers had to move her body from the cemetery to another location as the space of the cemetery was needed for building a new dam. When the body of the girl was unearthed it was found to every body's astonishment that the body was still intact and completely weightless. The villagers decided that she must be a saint and they raised funds to send Margarito to Rome. The narrator finds little hope in materializing the process of sainthood and eventually loses contact with the man. After twenty two years the narrator has the occasion to meet the man again in Rome, still waiting patiently for Pope's approval. By the time four Popes had breathed their last and there was in fact no progress in the process. The narrator ends his story with the observation that Margarito, who has already spent twenty two years of his life fighting for his daughter's canonization, has in fact legitimate cause of his own canonization. As in other stories dealing with the simplicity of the common folk, here also the author lays bare the strength of the poor man's will and faith as well as his tenacity.

The story 'I Sell My Dreams' is about a woman whose dreams had oracular qualities since her childhood. As she became a young lady, she used this quality for earning money and became very rich. The narrator had the opportunity to verify the oracular quality of her dream. One night she told him to leave Vienna immediately and the narrator boarded the last train to Rome that night and luckily escaped a misfortune, Another time when the narrator was spending some days with Pablo Neruda, both of them had the occasion to see that woman by chance and after a day or two Neruda told him that he had dreamt about her. Later, after Neruda's departure, the narrator met the woman who told, "I dreamed he (Neruda) was dreaming about me." Since that day the narrator had never met her again. After years when he was having breakfast at Havana Riviera Hotel, suddenly a gigantic wave crushed down on the shore and picked up several cars and much to his astonishment he found the smashed body of that woman under one of the smashed cars. It was the gold ring shaped like a snake in his right forefinger, one that she had always been wearing, was the mark of identification. The narrator asked the Portuguese ambassador with whom she had come what she was doing. The ambassador answered with certain disenchantment "Nothing. She dreamed." The story points at the irony that the woman who could save other's life with the help of the oracular quality of her dreams fails to save her own life from natural disaster. The story 'The Ghost of August' is a simple ghost story in which a family spending holidays in Tuscany decides to spend the night in a castle owned by a friend and has a horrifying experience. They learnt that the builder of the castle Ledovico, a renaissance nobleman, killed his bride in bed, before setting his dogs on himself and each night that murder is enacted in their bed room. The family disregarded the story as fake and slept in a guest room only to awake in the bedchamber of Lodovico, with fresh bloods on the sheets and a scent of fresh strawberries in the air. 'Maria dos Prazeres' is a reflection on solitude while 'The Trail of Your Blood in the Snow' focuses on the death of a newly-wed woman who scraps her ring finger in a rose thorn and the profuse bleeding that starts never stops. Billy Sanchez and Nena Daconle, both children of wealthy Colombian families, fly to Europe to celebrate their honeymoon. When Nena's scar continues to bleed profusely, she is admitted to the ICU of a Paris hospital. As per the rules of the hospital, a patient may be visited once a week and Billy fails to arrange a meeting with Nena earlier. When he goes to the hospital after a week, he learns that she bled to death sixty hours after admission. Nena's parents already sent her body home for burial. Billy exits the hospital with thoughts of violence and revenge for his calamity.

Marquez's stories range from formal experiments with form to delineation of themes and motifs which are the characteristic qualities of his fiction. While 'One of These Days' is a superb example of an ironic presentation of the rule of violence in Latin America and the story deserves attention for its brevity, 'A Very Old Man with Enormous Wings' is a perfect example of 'magic realism.' 'Death Constant beyond Love' presents romantic love in a typical Marquez style while 'Big Mama's Funeral' expresses his hatred towards dictatorship through exaggerated rendering of facts. Marquez is also criticized for dealing with melodramatic incidents which go against the decorum of short story. He did this intentionally as he felt an intense urge for revealing the inhuman oppression during dictator's rule and to give a violent shake to the complacent mind exposing the exact nature of torture inflicted on the women folk.

Notes

1 The French, led by their imperialist zeal in the nineteenth century, coined the term 'Latin America,' opposing Latin to Anglo America to claim for political gain a historical and linguistic kinship with regions recently freed from Spanish domination. Although there was little cultural connection between the region and the Roman Empire, the term began to be widely used, despite constant debates in regard to its justification and proposal of other terms such as 'Iberoamerica,' 'Hispanoamerica' and 'Indoamerica' for the entire continent. After the removal of Spanish rule when the continent was suffering from political unrest, intellectuals and writers from all over the region, most of who were banished, often met in Paris where they sought for a common platform and because of their connections with France they did not much bother about the coinage of the term.

2 Introduction to The Oxford Book of *Latin American Short Stories* ed. Roberto Gonzalez Echevarria (Oxford University Press; 1999), p.11

3 Ibid. p. 5

4 The new writers of Latin America who assembled in Paris began to publish anthologies that included works by writers from several countries of the continent. The first of these was *America Poetica*, compiled by the Argentinean Juan Maria Gutierrez which appeared in Chile in 1846.

History, Mundane Reality and Fantasy in Marquez's Fiction

While Marquez's stories are noted for their elements of fantasy woven into otherwise realistic setting, and the fantastic elements are rendered as things that happen every day, there being hardly any sense of awe either in the narrator's rendering of events or in the characters' reactions to them, his novels are noted for their magnificent design that focuses on some basically realistic event—be it an event of war or of love and lack of love generating solitude—and the design is woven out of historical facts and elements taken from folk tales and legends. In his 1982 Nobel Prize Acceptance speech, he refers to all the former colonies of Spain in Latin America from Colombia to Cuba and in his fictional writings he exhibits the struggle of the entire nation for coming to terms with the history of the land.[1] And he does so through a unique interweaving of fact and fiction—of journalistic accounts of gross horror of colonial plunder and the subsequent rule of dictators narrated in the manner of a folk tale that renders fantasy in a way as if it is experienced as fact.

To start with his celebrated novel *One Hundred Years of Solitude* (first published in original Spanish under the title *Cien Anos de Soledad* in 1967); this is the best example of his drawing liberally from the history of Colombia and the past of the continent at large, from the colonial times and the war of independence to the time of Civil War.[2] The historical event of foreign invasion in sixteenth century is presented through Ursula's recollections in the second chapter (the divisions are not however referred to as chapters) of the novel. "When the pirate

Sir Francis Drake attacked Riohacha in the sixteenth century, Ursula Iguaran's great-great-grandmother became so frightened with the ringing of alarm bells and the firing of canons that she lost control of her nerves and sat down on a lighted stove . . .she did not dare fall asleep." (23). The family had to wind up their business and to settle in a peaceful Indians located village in a distant area where they established a partnership business with a native-born tobacco planter, Don Jose Arcadio Buendia. Centuries later a man of the tobacco planter's family, Jose Arcadio Buendia, married the Aragonese daughter Ursula and they were products of "two races that had interbred over the centuries" (24). Thus Marquez made free use of history, projecting the invaders as the root cause behind dislocation and sufferings attached to it. History and fantasy are blended in the description of Sir Francis Drake's crocodile hunting with canons and his stuffing them "with straw to bring to Queen Elizabeth" (16) and in the description of the "soft-skinned cetaceans that had the head and torso of a woman, causing the ruination of sailors" (16). In his Nobel Prize acceptance speech Marquez traces the origin of the fantasies attached to the Caribbean region to the writings of Antonio Pigarfetta, a Florentine navigator, who after his voyage around the world including the Southern parts of America gave "strictly faithful account that nonetheless resembles a venture into fantasy." To quote from the speech, "He wrote of having seen a misbegotten creature with the head and ears of a mule, a camel's body, the legs of a dear and the whinny of a horse. . . . This short and fascinating book, which even then contained the seeds of our present day novels, is by no means the most staggering account of our reality in that age" (*www.nobelprize.org./nobel prizes/ literature/1982marquez-lecture.html.)*.

The focus of the novel is however on the Civil War: along with journalistic report of the conflicts between the Liberals and the Conservatives, there are other descriptions related to the setting, the establishment of the locality Macondo and the extended family of its founder, Jose Arcadio Buendia whose son Aureliano Buendia became Colonel and the most celebrated leader of the Liberal party. Before describing the Civil War, the phrase "facing the firing squad," referring to the Civil War, is used several times, as refrains in a poem, in connection with other events. The very first line of the novel refers to Colonel Aureliano Buendia's remembrance of his childhood—of his father's discovery of ice—at the time of his facing firing squad and then the entire chapter concentrates on the father's activities—his establishment of a new locality, his contact with the gypsies, his knack for alchemy and the tragic end of his life. In the family photograph taken by Melquiades, Aureliano appeared in black velvet. "He had the same languor and same clairvoyant look that he would have years later as he faced the firing squad" (48). Next, while describing the death of the old gypsy Melquiades, Arcadio's remembering the incident at the time of facing firing squad is referred: "Years later, facing the firing squad, Arcadio would remember the trembling with which Melquiades made him listen to several pages of his impenetrable writing, which of course he did not understand, but which when read aloud were like encyclicals being chanted" (66). Again, firing squad is referred to in connection with Aureliano Buendia's marriage: "Aureliano, dressed in black, wearing the same patent leather boots with metal fasteners that he would have on a few years later as he faced the firing squad, had an intense paleness. . ." (72). Remedios was the last person "Arcadio thought about a few years later when he faced the firing squad" (78). Thus from the very beginning of the novel the Civil War is projected as the centre of attention.

While the Civil War forms the centre of the novel, the incidents in the life of Jose Arcadio Buendia, rendered as part of an epic design, offer the background of the land that was to be devastated by Civil War. In order to underscore its difference from a realistic novel, *One Hundred Years of Solitude* is given a 'once upon a time ambience' in the very beginning, while revealing the history of the land: "Many years later . . . Colonel Aureliano Buendia was to remember that distant afternoon when his father took him to discover ice." Without referring to any specific time the line takes the reader back to a "distant" past, and the place referred to as backdrop, 'Macondo,' the reconstruction of the author's birthplace Aracataca, is not to be found anywhere in world map. The small village's alienation from the outer world of mechanical invention is revealed through the wondrous reactions of Jose Arcadio Buendia when he saw a piece of magnet or a magnifying glass. Ignoring his wife Ursula's suggestions and much to her agony, Jose Arcadio Buendia purchased from the wandering gypsies piece of magnet in exchange of his mule and a pair of goats, animals that supported their poor domestic holdings, and a magnifying glass in exchange of three colonial gold coins, which had been buried under Ursula's bed as a treasure. A man of rich imagination, he used the magnet for drawing gold from underground and hoped that the magnifying glass could be used for destroying enemies from afar and the device would be purchased by the government. Both the projects failed much to his financial loss but his spirit was indomitable. He spent his nights watching the course of the stars and almost contracted sunstroke while trying to establish an exact method to ascertain noon. When he became an expert in the use of his instruments, he conceived a notion of space that allowed him to navigate across unknown seas. When he revealed his discovery that the earth is round like an orange, everybody thought that he was out of his reason. Melquiades, one of the intelligent gypsies of the old order, returned to set things right. He gave public praise to the intelligence of a man who from pure astronomical speculation had evolved a theory that had already been proved in practice, although unknown in Macondo until then. As a proof of his admiration he offered to set up a laboratory of an alchemist for him. His capacity to found a new village has also been revealed in an elaborate way. He also offered a beautiful plan of the new settlement and kept the village hygienic so that there was no premature death. "Jose Arcadio Buendia, . . . had set up the placement of the houses in such a way that from all of them one could reach the river and draw water with the same effort, and he had lined up the streets with such good sense that no house got more sun than another during the hot time of day. Within a few years Macondo was a village that was more orderly and hardworking than any known until then by its three hundred inhabitants. It was a truly happy village where no one was over thirty years of age and where no one had died" (15). The gypsies, who exploited the simple villagers like Jose Arcadio Buendia, may be interpreted as the colonial rulers who plundered the land while Melquiades stands for a number of white men who stayed in the land and helped the people with their scientific knowledge. The founder of Macondo also falsifies the claim of the Europeans that they were the only civilized race in the world. Through the rich imagination, intelligence and organizing capacity of Jose Arcadio Buendia Marquez seeks to highlight the rich culture of the region which has always been ignored and also obliterated by the Europeans.

Jose Arcadio Buendia's encounter with the newly appointed magistrate Don Apolinar Moscot, who had been sent as the representative of the new ruler staying in capital far from Macondo, is another instance of his courage as well as the meaningless and oppressive process of ruling. When their new house built under Ursula's supervision was complete, she had an official order to paint the front blue and not white as they wanted. Marquez's ironic presentation of the magistrate and his office at once reveals the new government's distance from the mass and its attempt to start a regime of horror. "He set up a table and a chair that he had brought from Jacob, nailed up on the wall the shield of the republic that he had brought with him, and on the door he painted the sign: 'Magistrate.' His first order was for all the houses to be painted blue in celebration of the anniversary of national independence" (53). Jose Arcadio Buendia told him that they needed no order with pieces of paper and that they needed no judge because there was nothing that could need judging. He also made it clear that if the magistrate would create disorder with his meaningless order of painting one's house blue, thereby intruding into the personal freedom of the people, he would have to leave the place. The magistrate's attempt to threaten Jose Arcadio Buendia with his words that he was armed only brought the opposite result as he was soon grabbed by the lapels and lifted from the ground and was carried in the middle of the road in that position. The magistrate left the place and came back again with his family and six barefoot soldiers carrying shotguns a week later. This time Jose Arcadio did not show his strength out of consideration for the mayor's wife and children but calmly asked him to send his soldiers and declared that everyone should have the freedom to color his house according to his own liking. The magistrate continued to stay and through his rule sowed the seeds of revolt and terrorism. Jose Arcadio Buendia, however, resigned to his work in the lab and finally got what he was looking for. He connected the mechanism of the clock to a mechanical ballerina, and the toy danced uninterruptedly to the rhythm of his own music for three days. He was so excited that he stopped eating and sleeping. During this time he conversed with the dead man Prudencio Aguilar—the man whom he had killed in a duel many years ago and who was often seen at night thirsty and full of pain after his death and it was his repeated arrival at night that led Jose Arcadio to leave his ancestral village and found Macondo—and this was their first encounter in Macondo. As Prudencio told him, he could not keep contact with him as no dead man could tell him anything about Jose Arcadio for Macondo was still a town unknown to the dead. This time Jose Arcadio was not suffering from a sense of sin and instead of avoiding him he accepted poor Prudencio as his old friend, both being in need of friendship. This visit though appears fantastic, is related to the deepest region of Jose Arcadio's mind: his past came back to him in form of hallucinations. He became crazy, as he himself said, but his craziness had its own logic. His project failed, as he explained, for the simple reason that a pendulum could lift anything into the air but it could not lift itself, and he had overlooked this simple fact before undertaking the project. His despair arose out of a serious philosophical concern: he failed to see any change in the passage of time, Tuesday or Wednesday being in no way different from Monday according to him. As his frustration led him to smash whatever he found, he was tied to the chestnut tree in their courtyard, looking like a tragic hero. Tied to the trunk of the tree, huddled on a wooden stool underneath the palm shelter, "the enormous old man, discoloured by sun and rain, made a vague smile of gratitude," when Remedios brought him a piece of their wedding cake. He could also have discourse in Latin with priest Nicanor who came to Macondo for the first time on the occasion of the marriage of Aureliano and Remedios and who decided to stay there for spreading Christianity. The priest talked to Jose Arcadio everyday "to inject the faith into his twisted mind," but Jose Arcadio demanded God's photograph as the only proof of his existence. All this reveals the unrecorded parts of the history of the colonial masters of Europe who sought to control the mass in their colonies with the help of Christianity.

It is rendered as a design of fate that Aureliano fell in love with the magistrate's beautiful daughter Remedios. The girl was very small but Aureliano was ready to wait for her for a long time. Aurelino almost left the work in the lab for his love and his gesture created jealousy and complexity in the household and those incidents are like the various subplots in an epic. Remedios's sudden and pathetic death was a great shock to

Aureliano but it did not produce the despair feared by him. It was rather a dull feeling of rage that gradually dissolved in a solitary and passive frustration. He plunged into his work again, but continued to visit Remedois's father, the magistrate, keeping up the custom of playing dominoes with him. While spending time with him in his room he came in contact with direct politics. "On one occasion on the eve of the elections, Don Apolinar Moscot returned from one of his frequent trips worried about the political situation in the country. The Liberals were determined to go to war. Since Aureliano at that time had very confused notions about the differences between the Conservatives and the Liberals, his father-in-law gave him some schematic lessons. The Liberals, he said, were Freemasons, bad people, wanting to hang priests, to institute civil marriage and divorce, to recognize the rights of illegitimate children as equal to those of legitimate ones, and to cut the country up into federal system that would take power away from the Supreme authority. The Conservatives, on the other hand, who had received their power directly from God, proposed the establishment of public order and family morality. They were the defenders of the faith of Christ, of the principle of authority, and were not prepared to permit the country to be broken down into autonomous entities" (84). Because of his humanitarian feelings Aureliano sympathized with the Liberal attitude with respect to the rights of the illegitimate children, but in any case, he could not understand how people could wage war over such things. He also could not understand why six soldiers under a sergeant were recruited by his father-in-law in a town that hardly showed political passions. Those soldiers went from house to house confiscating hunting weapons, machetes and even kitchen knives before they distributed among males over twenty-one the blue ballots with the names of the Conservative candidates and the red ballots with the names of the Liberal candidates. On the eve of the elections the magistrate himself read a decree that prohibited the sale of alcoholic beverages and gathering together of more than three people who were not of the same family. The elections took place without incident. Aurelino saw that the voting was absolutely free and fare. At four in the afternoon a roll of drums in the square announced the closing of the polls and the magistrate sealed the ballot box with a label crossed by his signature. That night while playing dominoes with Aureliano, he ordered the sergeant to break the seal of the ballot box in order to count the votes. "There were almost as many red ballots as blue, but the sergeant left only ten red ones and made up the difference with blue ones. Then they sealed the box again with a new label and the first thing on the following day it was taken to the capital of the province" (85). It was now exposed to Aureliano why the Liberals would start war and he could not help himself uttering that if he were a liberal, he would go to war. Thereon the magistrate replied that the switching of the ballots was done before him for he was certain that his son-in-law was not a Liberal. In fact, the town did not much bother about the result of the election but about the fact the soldiers had not returned the weapons. A group of women spoke with Aureliano so that he could ask his father-in-law for the return of their kitchen knives. The magistrate told him in confidence that the soldiers had taken the weapons including the knives as proof that the Liberals had collected weapons for war. The cynicism of the remark alarmed him and he kept silence. But one day when he was in company of his friends who were discussing about the return of the knives he was asked by one whether he was a Liberal or a Conservative. He replied that if he would have to be something, then he would be a Liberal. His friends wasted no time to send him to Dr. Noguera, who was in reality a charlatan. "Behind his innocent faced of a doctor without prestige there was hidden a terrorist who with his short legged boots covered his scars that five years in the stocks had left on his legs" (86). The background of the Civil War as well as Aureliano Buendia's joining the Liberal

Party after the exposure of the Conservative Party's secret method of destroying the opponent is rendered in a brief and rather dramatic way. Basically a poet and a lover, Aureliano was drawn to the Liberal party but could not at first follow the party's ideology as dictated by Dr. Noguera, the leader in disguise. But the Conservative party's rule of terror soon turned him into a rebel. The narrator describes the event in a perfect journalistic way: "War, in fact, had broken out three months before. Martial law was in effect in the whole of the country. The only one who knew it immediately was Don Apolinar Moscote, but he did not give the news even to his wife while the army platoon that was to occupy the town by surprise was on its way. They entered noiselessly before dawn, with two pieces of light artillery drawn by mules, and they set up their headquarters in the school. At 6 p.m. curfew was imposed. A more drastic search than the previous one was undertaken, house by house; they dragged out Dr. Noguera, tied him to a tree in the square, and shot him without any due process of law. . .The decisions were made by the army captain, who each morning collected an extraordinary levy for the defiance of public order. Four soldiers under his command snatched a woman who had been bitten by a mad dog from her family and killed her with their rifle butts" (88-89). Aureliano Buendia took no more time to decide. "Tuesday at midnight in a mad operation, twenty-one men under the age of thirty commanded by Aurelanio Buendia, armed with table knives and sharpened tools, took the garrison by surprise, seized the weapons, and in the courtyard executed the captain and the four soldiers who had killed the woman"(89).

Once Aureliano joined the Liberal party, which was then a group of rebels engaged in secret war against the government, there was no turning back. The narrator of the novel supplies brief report of the conflict in a perfectly dispassionate way. "A short time later contradictory news of the war began to come in. While the government itself admitted the progress of the rebellion, the officers in Macondo had confidential reports of the imminence of a negotiated peace. . .Ten days after a joint communiqué by the government and the opposition announced the end of the war, there was news of the first uprising of Colonel Aureliano Buendia on the western border" (122-23). A combination of politics, journalism and anecdotal literature is evident in the extracts quoted above. With his unique sense of journalistic neutrality the narrator presents both the official and the unofficial news in one sentence: "While the government announced that it was maintaining control throughout the country, the Liberals were receiving secret news of armed uprisings in the interior. The regime would not admit a state of war until it was proclaimed in a decree that had followed a court-martial which had condemned Colonel Aureliano Buendia to death in absentia"(131). The government, however, did not dare to execute Aurelanio Buendia for fear of further aggression of the Liberals and after his release his men proclaimed him to be the chief of the revolutionary forces of the Caribbean coast. Soon a message from the government announcing the death of the Colonel was sent all over the country and after two days a multiple telegram was sent announcing another uprising on the southern plains. That was how the legend of the ubiquitous Colonel Aureliano Buendia began. And as the war became more intense and widespread, Aureliano Buendia's "image was fading into a universe of unreality" (136). The author yet presents him as a person of flesh and blood who changes a lot when assigned immense power. There was indeed a lot of change in the character of Aureliano; he became aggressive, lost all poetic qualities and got much engaged in satisfying his sensuality. Two months later when he returned to Macondo, "his upset was changed to stupefaction." Even Ursula was surprised at how much he had changed. He came with no noise, no escort, wrapped in a cloak in spite of the heat, and with three mistresses, whom he installed in the same house, where he spent most of his time lying in a hammock. He had not returned to reading his poetry, which filled more than five volumes and lay forgotten at the bottom of his trunk. He scarcely read the telegraphic dispatches that reported routine operation and even did not bother about the internal conflicts in the party. That internal crisis was perhaps the most critical moment of the war. The Liberal landowners, who had supported the revolution in the beginning, made secret alliances with the Conservative landowners in order to stop the revision of property titles. The politicians who had supplied funds for the war from exile publicly repudiated the drastic aims of Colonel Aureliano Buendia, but even that withdrawal of authorization did not seem to bother him. At first, intoxicated by the glory of his return, by his remarkable victories, he had peeped into the abyss of greatness, declaring that no human being, not even Ursula, could come closer to him than ten feet. The first time that he was in Manaure after the shooting of General Moncada, he hastened to fulfill his victim's last wish returning his personal things such as medal and ring to his widow who did not allow him to enter her house. Though the Colonel showed no sign of anger, the widow's house was sacked by his bodyguards and reduced to ashes. Colonel Gerineldo had the courage to criticize Aureliano as he said that Aureliano was rotting alive. About this time Colonel Aureliano called together a second assembly of the principal rebel commanders. The author gives details of that meeting, exposing the way a leader turns autocratic after consuming power and how most of the activists remain unaware of what is actually going on. "He found all types: idealists, ambitious people, adventurers, those with social resentments, even common criminals. There was even a former Conservative functionary who had taken refuge in the revolt to escape a judgment for misappropriation of funds. Many of them did not know why they were fighting" (139). The differences of values among all those men who assembled were on the verge of causing an internal explosion. Aureliano's aim was to unify the rebels and as he found it impossible to tame all of them, the untamed ones were cut to bits by matches in ambush, though there was no written order anywhere. Colonel Aureliano Buendia thus assumed absolute power and the author shows how the intoxication of power began to break apart under waves of discomfort: "Lost in the solitude of his immense power, he began to lose direction. He was bothered by the people who cheered him in neighboring villages, and he imagined that they were the same cheers they gave the enemy. . . He felt scattered about, multiplied, and more solitary than ever. He was convinced that his own officers were lying to him" (140). The description of Aureliano's abuse of power provided here holds up not only a true picture of the political condition of Latin America but also of the third world countries where ideology is only the lip service of the politicians and the only thing they aspire is absolute power. Marquez's success lies in depicting this rotten picture along with an in-depth study of the psyche of the man in absolute power: "Alone, abandoned by his premonitions, fleeing the chill that was to accompany him until death, he sought a last refuge in Macondo in the warmth of his oldest memories" (140). In Macondo his solitude was not removed in any way, the aura of legend that glowed about his presence, having changed him into a stranger. "Colonel Aureliano Buendia scratched for many hours trying to break the hard shell of his solitude. His only happy moments, since that immense afternoon when his father had taken him to see ice, had taken place in his silver workshop where he passed the time putting little gold fishes together. He had had to start thirty-two wars and had had to violate all of his pacts with death and wallow like a hog in the dung heap of glory in order to discover the privileges of simplicity almost forty years later" (142). He was strongly criticized by his party men for making peace treaty with the Conservative government. Ultimately his despair led to commit suicide but his attempt failed. The failure of his death brought back his lost prestige. The same people who invented the story that he had sold the war for a room with walls made of gold bricks, defined the attempt at suicide as an act of honour and proclaimed him a martyr. The ageing and disillusioned Colonel was slowly losing all contact with the reality of the nation. Enclosed in his workshop, his only relation with the rest of the world was his business in little gold fishes. One of the soldiers who had guarded his house during the first days of peace would sell them in the villages of the swamp and return with coins and news. It was learnt from him that the Conservative government, with the backing of the liberals, was reforming the calendar so that each president could remain in power for one hundred years. Marquez's close study of dictatorship in different Latin American countries is revealed in such hyperbolic statements in which fantasy is blended with stark reality.

After Colonel Aureliano Buendia it was the turn of the next generation of the extended Buendia family, most of them illegitimate sons of Aureliano Buendia and his brother, to join the Liberal Party. The arrival of the foreigners for business along with the automobiles, cinema and other gadgets brought a sea change in Macondo and made the political situation more complex. The proposal of banana plantation in the enchanted region that Jose Arcadio Buendia and his men had crossed in search of the roots to the great invention was a curse in disguise, as their sole intention was plunders through threatening.[3] "When the banana company arrived, however, the local functionaries were replaced by dictatorial foreigners whom Mr. Brown brought to live in the electrified chicken yard so that they could enjoy, as he explained it, the dignity that their status warranted and so that they would not suffer from the heat and the mosquitoes and the countless discomforts and privations of the town. The old policemen were replaced by hired assassins with machetes" (196). The torture inflicted by the policemen of

Banana Company on the common people was unthinkable. During that time a brother of the forgotten Colonel Magnifico Visbal was taking his seven year old grandson to get soft drink at one of the pushcarts on the squire. As the child accidentally bumped into a corporal of police and spilled the drink on his uniform, the policeman cut him to pieces with his machete, and with one stroke he cut off the head of the grandfather as he tried to stop him. The whole town saw the decapitated man pass by as a group of men carried him to his house, with a woman dragging the head by its hair, and the bloody sack with the pieces of the child. Such a horrifying incident, never officially recorded anywhere, opens up the dirty colonial face of USA, as the banana company was an American fruit company. In the guise of business it was the intrusion of imperial powers in Macondo, the powers that first took the government and the people in confidence, harnessing improvement in the region. Its exploitation of the land was manifold. They occupied the land for their own benefit, kept the common people in an awe-stricken atmosphere and deprived the laborers engaged in plantation of their dues. The laborers went on strike and the owners of the company used their force as well tactics to punish the disobedient laborers. The author offers dispassionate rendering of the strike and its aftermath which could very well be extracts from a daily news paper: "The great strike broke out. Cultivation stopped halfway. . . . The idle workers overflowed the towns. . . . Martial law enabled the army to assume the functions of arbitrator in the controversy, but no effort of conciliation was made . . . the soldiers cut and loaded the bananas and started the trains running. The workers. . .burned plantation and commissaries, tore up tracks to impede the passage of the trains. . .The situation was threatening to lead to a bloody and unequal civil war" (246-47). Mr. Brown, the manager of the banana company was taken out of Macondo in a safe place along with his family and other countrymen. They were kept under the protection of the army. The authorities called upon the workers to gather in Macondo. The summons announced that the civil and military leaders of the province would intercede in the conflict. Jose Arcadio Segundo who had taken part in a meeting of union leaders and had been commissioned, was in the crowd that had gathered at the station. He did not feel well as he noticed that the army had set up machine gun emplacements around the small square and that the wired city of the banana company was protected by artillery pieces. Around twelve o'clock, waiting for a train that was not arriving, more than three thousand people, workers, women, and children, had spilled out of the open space in front of the station and were pressing into the neighboring streets, which the army had closed off with rows of machine guns. After a long waiting when the rumor came that the official train would not arrive until the following day, the crowd were disappointed. Then an army lieutenant climbed up on to the roof of the station where there were four machine gun emplacements and called for silence. Then followed the reading of decree that declared the strikers to be "bunch of hoodlums" and authorized the army to shoot. The narrator offers the most horrifying description of murder that could be imagined. The assembled people were "swept down by the wave of bullets" (249). The survivors tried to go back to the small Square. "They were penned in, swirling about in a gigantic whirlwind that little by little was being reduced to its epicenter as the edges were systematically being cut off all around like an onion being peeled by the insatiable and methodical shears of the machine guns" (249). Corpses were then piled up "in the same way in which they transported bunches of bananas" (250). Jose Arcadio Segundo, being unconscious was also carried in train along with the corpses. When he came to his senses he gradually realized his condition. Trying to flee from the nightmare, he dragged himself from one car to another in the direction in which the train was heading, and in the flashes of light that broke through the wooden slats he saw the corpses of men, women and children who would be thrown into the sea like rejected bananas. He recognized one woman who sold drinks in the squire. When he got to the first car he jumped into the darkness and lay beside the tracks until the train had passed. It was the longest one he had ever seen, with almost two hundred freight cars and a locomotive in either end and a third in the middle. It had no lights, not even the red and green running lights, and it slipped off with a nocturnal and stealthy velocity. On the top of the cars there could be seen the dark shapes of the soldiers with their machine guns. Next morning when Jose Arcadio Segundo managed to reach a locality on his way to Macondo and gathered the energy to utter that at least three thousand people had been killed, a lady who offered him a mug of coffee on request, told him with a pitying look that since the time of Colonel Aureliano Buendia nothing had happened. Nobody believed in the version of the massacre or the nightmare trip of the train loaded with corpses travelling towards the sea. The night before there was an extraordinary proclamation to the nation which said that the workers assembled for the meeting had left the station and had returned to their homes in peaceful groups. The proclamation also stated that the union leaders, with great patriotic spirit, had reduced their demands to two points: a reform of medical services and the building of latrines in the living quarters. It was also declared later that the military authorities obtained the agreement with the workers and they hastened to tell Mr. Brown who accepted the new condition and also offered to pay for three days of public festivities to celebrate the end of the conflict. Without expressing utter disgust at this planned massacre and the obliteration of the massacre from all records, the narrator reports the happenings with journalistic skill, keeping his calm. "The official version, repeated a thousand times and mangled out all over the country by every means of communication the government found at hand, was finally accepted: there was no dead, the satisfied workers had gone back to their families, and the banana company was suspending all activity until the rain stopped. Martial law continued with an eye to the necessity of taking emergency measures for the public disaster of the endless downpour, but the troops were confined to quarters" (252). Thus the method of successful reporting and a depth of vision enabled the author to present hard reality that has a look of unreality. The qualities of journalistic writing—an impersonal and dispassionate rendering of matters in sentences devoid of all ornaments—are visible in the author's attempt to record the real incidents that had been erased from all official records.

The revelation of such horrifying historical events has a mesmerizing effect on the readers. Thanks to the author's unique art of narration, which includes elements from legends and folk tales in a naïve way and weaves a design that is close to that of an epic, the novel with its "extraordinary events of a century" becomes a classic of the grandest scale. The use of fantasy not only lessens the impact of terrifying events on the reader's mind while making those events more prominent through contrast but also reveals the exact psychological condition which may not be revealed through mere realistic description. For example, when Ursula left home in search of her eldest son Jose Arcadio, who had gone with the gypsies, leaving her husband and the second son busy in their laboratory and her little daughter to the care of a woman, it was found that an empty mug became too heavy to be removed, a pan of water on the worktable boiled without any fire under it, a basket began to move by itself. The disorder in the family during the housewife's absence could hardly be better expressed. When Colonel Aureliano Buendia shot himself out of despair—he was saved however by mistake—his mother Ursula found a pot of milk full of worms in her kitchen. Again, after Jose Arcadio was shot dead in his house, a trickle of blood came out under the door and went out into the street and after crossing a long way reached Ursula's kitchen, enabling her to follow the thread of blood and reach the place where her son lay face down on the ground. All these are suggestive of Ursula's strong nerves, her deep concern for her sons and her presence of mind. Jose Arcadio Buendia's meeting with the dead man Prudencio Aguilar as well as Ursula's offering him water may be interpreted in terms of hallucinations and such incident reminds us of Macbeth and Lady Macbeth. A light rain of tiny little flowers falling on the dead body of Jose Arcadio Buendia and covering the streets of Macondo is of course a fantastic incident but it is a common one in legends and folktales used while describing the demise of a pure soul. There are occasional references to continuous rainfall and continuous lack of rain in Macondo which suggest a massive influx of easy money through business and dearth of money. For example, Fernanda's extravagant life is described as she had spent all her life in a way as if it had been raining. To quote the lines that reveal Macondo's distress after the Fruit Company's systematic plunder of the resources of the land: "One Friday at two in the afternoon the world lighted up with a crazy crimson sun as harsh as brick dust and almost as cool as water, and it did not rain again for ten years. Macondo was in ruins. In the swampy streets there were the remains of the furniture, animal skeletons covered with red lilies, the last memories of the hordes of newcomers who had fled Macondo as wildly as they arrived. The houses that had been built with such haste during the banana fever had been abandoned. The banana company tore down its installations. All that remained of the former wired-in city were the ruins. The wooden houses, the cool terraces for breezy card-playing afternoons, seemed to have been blown away in an anticipation of the prophetic wind that years later would wipe Macondo off the face of the earth" (268). Here is history of the wretched land, no fantasy. Marquez told in an interview that the incident of Remedios the Beauty flying up in air was taken from the description of a mother in his locality who told others that her daughter had miraculously been taken away by a whirlwind. The mother took the help of fantasy to cover up her daughter's elopement that was a shame to the family. In the novel the incident is rendered rather ironically as it is made clear that it was seen only by Ursula "who was almost blind at the time and. . .was sufficiently calm to identify the nature of that determined wind. . .as she watched Remdios the Beauty waving goodbye in the midst of the flapping sheets that rose up with her" (195). The use of such fantastic events exposes the deceptive nature of the society which was full of illegitimate children and prostitutes but which imposed restrictions on the women in upper class. Fantasy also helps the creation of epic grandeur in the novel: the fierce temerity with which Jose Arcadio Buendia had crossed the mountains to found Macondo and his zeal for discovery, the blind pride with which Colonel Aureliano Buendia undertook his fruitless wars and his capacity to love and to write poems, the mad tenacity with which Ursula watched over the survival of the line and Aureliano Segundo's looking for Fernanda without a single moment of respite are all evidences of epic design. Fatalism, as indicated in foretelling future events, adds to this grand effect. The prediction that the founder of the Buendia family would die tied up in a tree and the last member would be eaten up by ants comes true much to the effect of arousing awe and wonder. To quote the lines when Amaranta Ursula's motherless child was discovered: "It (the child) was a dry and bloated bag of skin that all the ants in the world were dragging towards their holes along the stone path in the garden. Aureliano could not move. Not because he was paralyzed by horror but because at that prodigious instant Melquiades' final keys were revealed to him and he saw the epigraph of the parchments perfectly placed in the order of man's time and space: *The first of the line is tied to a tree and the last is being eaten by the ants*" (334). Here is delineation of life's mystery which is universal.

One Hundred Years of Solitude records not only the political history of Colombia during the nineteenth and early twentieth century but also its cultural history as it emerged out of its primitive condition, consuming elements from variety of sources. Jose Arcadio Buendia's crossing the mountains in search of a new land for settlement places him and his race bracketed with any nomadic tribe of the ancient days. It being a permissive society the people of this tribe came in contact with other groups of people whose blood got mixed with theirs and developed a hybrid culture. As Widow Asis says to his son in *In Evil Hour,* Asises were the founders of the town, when they were nothing but swineherds, and they seemed to have blood that was sweet for gossip. What Widow Asis says may also be applicable to the Buendias in *One Hundred Years of Solitude.* The first foreigners in Macondo who are generally called 'gypsies' are likely to be Arabic or Spanish or Portuguese people some of whom like Melaquides settled in Macondo. Marquez was biased neither against the native Indian nor against the outsiders, the Arabic or the Spanish. He rendered the interaction of different races as a natural historical process, a process of evolution. While some writers like the Uruguayan Jose Enrique Rodo differentiated between gross sensuality and 'the noble and winged parts of the spirit,' Marquez did not believe in any such differences. Rather he felt that the so called 'barbarians' had an authenticity and spontaneity which would finally be more valuable for the continent. That is why the sensuality which characterizes the native Indians is never condemned in his work. Yet he did not disclaim the heritage of Spain by evoking an ideal vision of the past. Hence Ursula gradually learns Spanish and enriches her personality. The character of Colonel Aureliano Buendia is therefore not projected as ideal figure, his faults having been mercilessly criticized by his mother. The first thing that Marquez opposed as is clearly revealed in his fiction is the materialistic and utilitarian value of 'the cold America of the north.'

Marquez's first novel *La Mala Hora,* though published in 1962, took much time to be translated into English by Gregory Rabassa as *In Evil Hour* and it got published only in 1979. It has an episodic structure where all the important characters, taken from different occupations, function as links between the different social groups and consequently between the different episodes in the novel. Set in a small unnamed town in Colombia, it reveals the time of mid-1950s, enmeshed in civil wars and bloody repressions, known as *la violencia*[4]. The town has recently recovered from a violent military coup and all the representatives of the government are seriously trying to bring order in the town through queer ways which bring ludicrous effect. The story, as Marquez told a friend, was based on a real event that had taken place in a remote river side village where lampoons raised by scandal-mongering people provoked fights and feuds among them, compelling a lot of people abandon the village. Marquez's exclusive vision of reality as well as his imaginative richness enabled him to weave a plot related to contemporary social and political facts based on this 'real event.' The novel starts with a juxtaposition of a scene of murder and a ludicrous scene of love of the aged judge of the town. Everything is presented dramatically: getting up from bed in early morning Cesar Montero became ready to get out riding on his mule, taking leave from his wife with the words that they would meet next Saturday, and saw a piece of paper stuck to the door of the house; he read it without dismounting and tore it to pieces; then he went to Pastor's house and called him by his name and as Pastor appeared, Cesar Montero "with his heels planted on the earthen floor and the shotgun at waist level pointed at him. . .then he clenched his teeth and, at the same time, the trigger" (8). The ludicrous event is about Judge Arcadio who had always boasted of having made love three times a night and who now "broke the cords of the mosquito netting that morning and fell to the floor with his wife at the supreme moment, wrapped up in the embroidered canopy" (20), and that too, as it was found later, keeping the front door wide open. Marquez uses his satire blended with wit and humor through the introduction of government officials in whimsical roles. The mayor had been suffering from acute toothache and that morning after getting up from bed when he was applying mentholated Vaseline on his cheek, he learned from an outside shouting that Cesar Montero had killed Pastor. He came out immediately taking revolver in his hand and found Montero on the Squire. Only after getting Montero under control he realized that he was wearing only his pajama bottoms. Surprisingly, before the proceedings started he told Father Angel that Montero was well known to him and that nothing was going to happen to him. He was so much obsessed with his thought of keeping everything in order, that he did not much bother about the incident of murder—it is revealed ironically that murder was never a new thing in the town—but seriously tried to follow the post murder formalities which were not maintained earlier. He asked the doctor to perform the autopsy of the dead body and ordered the judge to get a body removal form. It was also thought a part of maintaining order that the movie show should be cancelled that night enabling everybody to join the mourning. The priest declared that the mayor had changed in the new regime. But the memory of recent past was strong in the mind of everybody. When the judge joined his office in his chamber with its wall newly decorated with a framed lithograph of the smiling president underneath a gilt inscription: *Peace and Justice*, the secretary told him how the previous Judge Viela had been killed for saying that he was there to guarantee the sanctity of the ballot. The manager of the cinema show, frustrated that he would have to bear the loss of cancelling a show, told how the year before a man had been killed while the film show was going on and the cinema show continued after the dead body had been removed from the place.

The cause behind the murder soon came out: the sheet of paper that Montero found on his doorstep was one of the wall posters full of scandals that plagued the town. It was written in that paper that Pastor the singer was in love with Montero's wife and he was so blind with rage that he did not even verify the matter and immediately killed the artist, who, as it is known soon, loved another woman Margot Ramirez whom he was to marry. Another lampoon affected Roberto who came to know about the scandal that his daughter Rebeca was not fathered by him. As Roberto was not like Montero, he discussed the matter with his mother the Widow Asis who asked him not to take such scandals seriously. However she appealed to the Father to take steps for finding out the culprits. The lampoon about Raquel Contreras was that the trips she took that year were not to get her dentures fitted but to get an abortion. When it is learnt that this was known to everybody, it becomes clear that in that rotten society one is allowed to do all sorts of incestuous deeds unless and until they are publicly exposed. The novel's chief concern is not however the moral laxity of the people but the political situation of the land which soon comes in the front and the issue of the lampoon that threatened all the well off persons in the town is not focused, the mystery of the authorship of the lampoon never being solved. But the lampoon issue is important from the point of view of the plot; it is the lampoon that caused the first murder and was also the cause behind imposing curfew with the return of which the political opposition seems also to be revived.

That the political situation of the land is in the center of the novel becomes clear in the conversation that goes on in the barbershop. The shop with its notice nailed to the back wall prohibiting any discussion on politics was in actuality a place for discussing matters connected only with politics. As the barber openly said to Mr. Carmichael, "A fine business: my party gets in power, the police threaten my political opponents with death, and I buy up their land and livestock at a price I set myself" (43). The barber also said that after the election he owned three towns, and in this way having raised his wealth he managed to get the upper hand even in case of the change of government. As Mr. Carmichael said that persecution having been over for a year, they need not talk about the same thing again and again, the barber replied, "The state of abandonment we're in is persecution too. . . . Abandoning us to God's mercy is another way of beating us up" (44). The barber also reminded the Syrian that his fellow countryman Elias's son got his four ribs broken on order of late Don Chepe Montiel. But the Syrian did not play on his tune, telling him that Elias was sorry for his son's involvement in politics and that his son was now having a grand time dancing in Brazil. There are references to the Liberal leader Colonel Aureliano Buendia who, on his way to Macondo to draw up the terms of surrender in the last civil war, had spent one night in a hotel in this town. The mayor's encounter with the dentist, whom he knew to be a revolutionary and to whom he had to go for pulling his aching tooth, there being no other option open to him in that small town, exposes the reality beneath the camouflage of peace. The mayor was accompanied by three armed soldiers when he went to the dentist's office. "With two quick charges they battered down the door with their rifle butts. They were already inside the house when the light in the vestibule went on. A small bald man with veins showing through his skin appeared in his shorts at the rear door, trying to put on his bathrobe. At the first instant he remained paralyzed with one arm up and his mouth open, as in the flash of a photograph. Then he gave a leap backward and bumped into his wife, who was coming out of the bed room in her night gown" (55-56). The lieutenant asked her not to move and she went back to the bed room. The dentist went towards the vestibule, tying the cord on his bathrobe, and at this time he could see three policemen, who were pointing their rifles at him, and the mayor, water dripping from all over his body, his hands in the pockets of his raincoat. The dentist walked to the dental office and the two police men went ahead of him to the door of the office. One turned on the light and the other went directly to the worktable and took a revolver out of the drawer. The mayor, who had entered last, behind the dentist, said that there must be another. The two policemen made a quick and conscientious search while the third guarded the door. They dumped the instrument box onto the work table, scattered plaster molds, unfinished false teeth, loose teeth and gold caps on the floor. They emptied the porcelain vials that were in the cabinet and making quick stabs with their bayonets, gutted the oilcloth cushion on the dentist's chair and the spring cushion on the revolving chair. The mayor told him that it would be better if the dentist would say where the revolver had been kept, for they had no intention to tear the house apart. The dentist's dull and narrow eyes behind his gold-framed glasses revealed nothing. He replied in a relaxed way that he was not in a hurry and that his house could as well be torn apart. After once more examining the room the mayor asked his men to stop searching. He stationed one by the street door, another at the entrance to the office and the third by the window. Then he settled his body on the chair and rested his skull on the headrest. The dentist picked some instruments up off the floor and put them in a pot to boil. When the water was boiling, he carried the pot over the table. As a policeman blocked his way, the dentist asked the mayor to order the policeman to change his place. The policeman moved away on a signal from the mayor. The dentist turned on the lamp and located the sick molar in the mayor's open mouth. As he got ready to pull the tooth, the mayor asked for applying anesthesia. The sharp, witty reply came from the dentist: "you people kill without anesthesia." As the mayor asked for anesthesia again, the dentist impatiently told that no anesthesia would work on such abscess. Having suffered the most terrible moment of his life the mayor got relaxed after the affected tooth was pulled. He then asked the policemen to get the instruments flung on the floor in order and the policemen did so. The mayor then asked them to leave. The dentist examined the mouth once again and took the light away. The mayor then accused the dentist of conspiracy and gave a small lecture on how he had saved the dentist earlier. "There were orders to level the house. . . There were precise instructions to *find* weapons and ammunition with the details of a nation-wide conspiracy . . . I thought I was doing the right thing by disobeying that order, but I was wrong. Things have changed now. The opposition has guarantees and everybody is living in peace, and still you go on thinking like a conspirator. . . . Your attitude is harmful to the town" (59-60). To justify his action the mayor also said that because of his stubbornness the town government would have to pay for the mess done by the policemen. The dentist, however, advised him to rinse his mouth with fenugreek water, ignoring what the mayor said to him. This satiric and funny presentation without any authorial remark exposes the real picture of fear, disbelief and terror even during the time of 'peaceful democracy.' Later, the mayor calls on the dentist alone on his way to the judge's house. As the dentist suggested that several cavities would have to be filled up, the mayor told that he would find some time for that. Thereon the dentist retorted that the mayor should come to see if the dentist's wish to have him die in his chamber came true. In a relaxed mood the mayor patted the dentist on his shoulder with the words that his teeth were above party politics.

While the mayor's encounter with the dentist reveals the environment of mutual disbelief and terror, his conversation with the murderer Cesar Montero exposes the corruption of taking bribe at the highest level of administration. It was decided that Montero would be taken to the capital for trial the next day and

Father Angel had already performed the ritual of confession. It was now the mayor's turn to deal with him. The mayor told him that having settled his accounts with God, Montero should now settle his account with the mayor. He tried to make Montero understand his position, clarifying how much he depended on the mayor for lessening his punishment. As the mayor told, a special investigator dealing with his case was likely to meet the mayor within two or three months and it was up to the mayor's sweet will then to fill him in. The mayor had the freedom, it is clear, to interpret Montero's crime in a manner that would obviously lessen his punishment. And to do so he must be compensated by Montero through hard cash. The mayor also cautioned him that he would have to pay at least twenty thousand pesos to the court and lawyers. Making a change in his tone he reminded Montero of the past when there were orders to murder him in ambush and confiscate his livestock to the government so that the government would have a way to pay off the enormous expenses of election in the whole department. Though other mayors in other towns had done such job, he did not do that, preferring to disobey the order of higher authority. As Montero seemed to be thinking at that moment, the mayor assured him with the words that he had not taken a single penny for himself from the amount Montero had spent for his life. "Everything was spent on organizing the elections. Now the new government has decided that there should be peace and guarantees for everybody and I go on being broke on my salary while you're filthy with money. You got yourself a good deal" (74). A shameless demand for money as is revealed here presents a true picture of taking bribe in the name of collecting funds for election not only in Latin America but also in all the 'democratic' countries of the third world. Montero simply asked the mayor how much and the immediate answer was five thousand pesos. Marquez's revelation of corruption through simple dramatic situations without using any authorial comment is simply superb. Towards the end of the novel, judge Arcadio, who had so far obeyed the mayor's orders ungrudgingly, says to the barber, "The lieutenant is sinking deep into the town. And he sinks in deeper everyday because he's discovered a pleasure from which there's no turning back: little by little, without making a lot of noise, he's getting rich" (156). The Barber is astonished to hear such comments from the judge as he had the notion that Judge Arcadio was friendly with the mayor. He now gives the hint that having made enough money the mayor is likely to leave the town. He also slipped a piece of paper in the Judge's pocket which the judge reads finding no other person present there, after the shaving is done. The barber quotes something from memory: "And still the same state of siege, the censorship of press, the same old officials. . ." (158). The fact that hardly anything has changed in the town after the change of government is clear in his musing.

Though the incidents in the novel move around the lampoons that disturb the lives of the dominant well off persons in the town, the plot is not based on the revelation of the mystery of the unknown culprit. For it does not matter who put those posters up. What matters is that the posters full of gossips did not reveal anything that was unknown to the people of the town. Some persons even wondered why so much trouble was taken to reveal some well circulated gossips. A man, for example, told Judge Arcadio about one such lampoon that it was seer foolishness: that the trips Raquel Contreras took that year were not to get her dentures fitted, as she said, but to get an abortion was already known to everybody. The author keeps the lampoons in the center of the novel in order to highlight the duplicity in the lives of the middle class people who do not much bother about their lack of morality unless and until this is publicly exhibited, much to their humiliation. Nor do these persons have the stamina to ignore their moral laxity publicly. The fortune teller Casandra's calculation in regard to the person behind fixing the lampoons is indeed thought provoking. "It's the whole town and it's nobody," she says (133). Moreover, these lampoons, though mere gossipy in nature and seem to have no capacity to disturb the law and order situation, prove to be disastrous only because the law and order situation in the town was not at all peaceful. The peace that was demanded to have been restored by the government was a fake one and that is why a little disturbance like spreading rumor brought disastrous effects. The first disaster, the murder of the singer Pastor, was committed by Cesar Montero whose immense wealth earned by his father in illegal ways had already been targeted by the most powerful persons in the town. One who is well aware of Cesar Montero's Othello-like nature, may very well calculate beforehand how infuriated that man might be after learning about his wife's infidelity and it was likely that he would undertake an honor killing. It is curious to note that the poor wife of Cesar who had once come to the town as a school teacher had to leave the town after Cesar's arrest and his mother, already troubled by her husband's ill-earned wealth, became crazy. In this situation it becomes easy to occupy the Montero's property only if Mr. Carmichael, the administrator of the family's affair, could be managed. And the mayor tried to manage him, keeping him under arrest for interrogation concerning the situation of the Montiel estate and at last revealing the proposal of buying the estate at a price fixed by the municipality. But with his inflexible determination not to permit it until the will is probated, Dr. Carmichael is quite a different type of person whom the mayor could not manage. Thanks to the lampoons, all these hidden plans and intentions came out, exposing the evil hour of the unknown town and also of similar hours in different parts of the world.

The novel ends with another incident related to the lampoons—the death of a young man in police custody who was accused of fixing the lampoons. Pepe Amador, a young man of about twenty with a "sharp and shallow pockmarked face" was arrested by the policemen for keeping a piece of paper which contained criticism of the present government. The mayor took an interview of the young man who was sitting on the concrete platform that served the prisoners as a bed. He did not ask the prisoner many questions; nor did he step into the cell. He kept looking on his pensive face and then shut the door and turning the key kept it in his pocket. He then examined the paper and was sure that it was the pamphlet of the rebel groups in Opposition. "So they have come back," he said to himself aloud. "They had come back. As before, they were mimeographed on both sides, and they could have been recognized anywhere and at any time by the indefinable mark of hesitation that clandestinely imprints" (145). The mayor took some time to decide his procedure and finally called a policeman whom he could trust and gave him the keys. The order he gave to the policeman makes it clear that the prisoner Pepe Amador would be accused of false charges as the rules in a democracy do not allow punishment for joining a political party other than the ruling one. The mayor said to the policeman, "Take charge of the boy. Try to convince him to give you the names of the ones bringing clandestine propaganda into town. If you cannot get them in a nice way, try any way you can to get him to talk" (146). As the policeman reminded him that the young man was on patrol that night for tracing the invisible person behind putting up lampoons, the mayor asked him not to bother about such things. He then ordered to send the men in the courtyard away and declared that there would be no patrol that night. The policemen taken into confidence by the mayor could catch the spirit of his order and Pepe Amador was killed next day. With an astonishing sense of calmness the narrator renders the event from the perspective of the mayor. "The mayor really did not find out what had happened until he moved aside the policemen who were blocking the entrance to the cell and saw Pepe Amador,

Lying on the floor, curled up, he had his hands between his thighs. He was pale, but there were no signs of blood. After convincing himself that there was no wound, the mayor laid the body out face up, tucked in the shirttail, and buttoned the fly. Finally he fashioned the belt. When he stood up he'd recovered his calm, but the expression with which he faced the policemen revealed a beginning of weariness" (175). He asked the policemen who had done the job and they accepted joint responsibility with their words "All of us." They also tried to justify their work by saying that Pepe had tried to escape. The mayor immediately said that that alibi would not work. The mayor was now thoughtful, obviously trying to get an explanation of the murder for avoiding the responsibility. As the mayor appeared in the door, Pepe's mother who had been breathing with a peaceful rhythm since her first howling like a dog, gave off a hoarse howl and shook with such violence that one of the policemen had to let her go and the other one pinned her to the ground with a wrestling hold. Without looking at the woman the mayor ordered the group that was witnessing the struggle to take the woman to her home to avoid something worse. After Pepe's mother was taken to her home, the town seemed 'peaceful.' The mayor then went straight to the dead man's cell. He had the policemen bring a piece of canvas and, with their help put the cap and the glasses on the corpse and wrapped it up. Then he collected some pieces of cord and wire and tied the body in a spiral form neck to ankles. He had a recovered look after finishing the work and ordered them to bring the shovel, the pick, and a lantern. He then asked the policemen to go to the rear courtyard, and dig a good deep hole where it was drier. Though it is clear by now what the mayor had intended, his order that everybody must remember for ever that the boy had never died but escaped makes his plan crystal clear. The mayor sought to obliterate all traces of the murder and wanted to project Pepe as the culprit behind the lampoons so that no one would doubt any political activity in the event. Quite understandably he took a u-turn when the doctor wanted to do the autopsy following his previous order. "There'll be no autopsy, since there's no dead body," he said clearly. Even when Father Angel told him that it was impossible to keep anything secret in that messy town, he simply repeated, "He escaped." This time it was hard for the mayor to stop them only with his words. Father Angel advanced two steps and the mayor remained planted with his legs apart to stop him. The doctor, with his voice hardened for the first time in a long while, told the mayor that autopsy had to be done and that they would clear up "the mystery of the fainting spells" the prisoners had in that jail. The mayor now started threatening them with the words that if they moved from where they were standing, he would shoot them off. He also declared that the little jokes being over, they were in war. With his final words that he liked that straight way of fighting, the doctor left the place, dragging Father Angel away by the sleeve. Henceforth nobody talked about lampoons. In the hubbub of the latest happenings they were nothing but a picturesque anecdote of the past. Father Angel is provided with the information of the latest happenings by the maid Mina who told that they lifted up the flooring of the barbershop and found guns. She also told that the jail was full and that men were going to the jungle to join up with guerrilla bands. The novel comes to its end with an unfinished sentence of Mina—"Last night, in spite of the curfew and in spite of the shooting. . ."—and her nervous smile of innocence. While the grim picture of evil hour provided in the novel offers a totally hopeless condition, Mina's innocent look and her unfinished sentence suggests a flicker of hope though in an insignificant way.

Critics' opinion in regard to *In Evil Hour* varies; some critics find this novel least affected by fantasy while others including the Nobel Laureate Mario Vergas Llosa interpret it as a fantastic text in which imagination works in a subtle way. It is however universally agreed that Marquez's capacity to expose the reality—the corruption in high places, dictatorial oppression under the mask of democracy, people's liking for gossiping and demoralizing other people and above all obliteration of facts by the government officials—is best revealed in this novel. And at the same time it cannot be denied that an air of unfathomable mystery hovers on the background from the very beginning. Comic exaggeration that increases the satiric effect, the use of incessant rain as symbol, unexpected behavior of the persons in high places such as the mayor's public appearance in underwear intensifies the atmosphere of mystery. In his continuous search for creating an alternative to the 'meat-and-potato' realism and the psychological realism in fiction, Marquez reaches at a point from where he finds that the same event which is a hard fact for one appears to be an extension of dream for another. When, for example, the mayor told Don Sabas that from that moment on, the cattle belonging to the estate of Jose Montiel were under the protection of the town government, Don Sabas, shaken by an interior laughter, told, "What a miracle. . .This all must seem like a dream to you"(163). Father Angel, disturbed by the troops of mice in the church and the frightful paralysis of the curfew in the town felt that all these plotted together so that he would be dragged by a blind force. The buzz of the harvest flies intensifying the solitude of the port, the smell of the rotten cow leaving an enormous gap in the atmosphere even after the cow was dragged off by the current (87), Toto Visbal's observation that "the whole country is patched up with cobwebs" (149) and such other descriptions add to the effect of creating a narrative mode that gathered elements from a variety of sources to oppose the realistic mode of writing.

No one Writes to the Colonel (Spanish *El coronel no tione quien le escriba* written between 1956-57 and published in 1961) was first published in its English form in USA by Harper and Row in 1968. This novella having hardly any fantastic event in it was the author's most favorite work for a long time. In his Memoir he explained that while writing this fictional work he had been inspired by his grandfather, who was also a colonel and who did not receive the pension he had been promised. The old Colonel in the novella lived with his ailing wife and the memory of their only son who had been killed, getting sustenance from the hope of the arrival of his pension papers from the government. The gray setting of the novel—a land devastated by dictatorship, internal war and loss of innumerable lives caused by civil war—is the factual rendering of the scenario as seen by the author in his childhood. The apparently insignificant incident of the colonel's preparation for attending the funeral of a musician in thc locality adds to the creation of the backdrop. "After shaving himself by touch—since he had lacked a mirror for a long time—the colonel dressed silently. His trousers, almost as tight on his legs as long underwear, closed at the ankles. . .When his wife told her it was as if he was dressed for some special event, he replied, 'This burial is a special event. It's the first death from natural causes which we've hade in many years'" (6). Without any authorial comment on the numbers of unusual death and the utter poverty of the common men, the above conversation offers a real picture of the post Civil war condition of Colombia. The image of Colonel's taking the tap off the coffee can that contained only a little spoonful of coffee reveals the picture of utter poverty that the Colonel and his ailing wife had been fighting for a long time, living on a meager amount of savings that too was running short. But each Friday was different, as this was the day of the arrival of postal peon in that remote village, for the post peon was the source of his hope for getting the letter of pension. Every Friday he went to the water side and wait for the motor launch that carried mail from the distant capital every weekend. And it became a regular show that the postman would shout from the launch, having seen the old man waiting by the river side that no one wrote to the

Colonel. The old fellow would then come back home to report to his wife that the longed-for letter had not yet arrived. When the old lady suffering from asthma, irritated and almost frustrated, would utter, "one must have the patience of an ox, as you do, to wait for a letter for fifteen years," the old man only reminded her calmly while reading the news paper that they would have to wait for their turn as their number was 1823. The woman's prompt reply was that since they had been waiting, that number would have come up twice in the lottery. The chief attraction of the novella is the character of the old man who reminds the readers of Hemingway and Samuel Beckett. He was eagerly waiting for the letter from the government which, besides removing his poverty was expected to give him an acknowledgement and honor. In spite of his fighting with poverty at this old age—he badly needed money for the medicine of his ailing wife—the Colonel is full of pride, never losing his hope. The author presents their suffering for a couple of months during winter when biting of cold and hunger become intolerable.

The old couple lost their only son who had been shot down at the cockfight "for disturbing clandestine literature." He had left a rooster which was both an asset and a liability for the Colonel. It was a liability as it had to be fed regularly while it was almost impossible to meet their own hunger, and it was an asset not only for being the last possession left by their son, but for raising the hope that it would win in the coming cock-fight season bringing honor to the Colonel as well as his village. Once in desperation the Colonel decided to sell the cock to the exploiter Sabas who was to give considerably less money than he had originally promised. But the villagers snatched the cock and entered it into trial fights, showing that the cock lived up to its reputation as a prize fighter. The Colonel changed his mind and gave the money back, concentrating on the hope raised by the rooster. He always ignored his wife's abusing comments in regard to the rooster and though exhausted—his bones aching from sleeplessness and his muscles tired of fasting—he attended the rooster, taking care of its needs. By the end of November he felt that the cock would die after two days without corn. Then he remembered a handful of beans which he had hung in the chimneys in July. He opened the pods and put down a can of dry seeds for the cock. The episode reaches its most touching part when the couple decided to sell stuff from their household, the things carrying memories of their good marriage and having been part and parcel of their married life, like the moth-eaten old umbrella which the wife had won in a ruffle many years ago. But they learned much to their astonishment that no one would buy their things as they had been outdated like themselves. Thc Colonel must have faced a crisis of identity and must have undergone a challenge to justify his own existence which, he must have felt by now, needed no official letter of acknowledgement.

The Autumn of the Patriarch (original Spanish title *El Otono del patriarca,* 1975) tells the story of a patriarch whom the people had not seen since the horrifying death of his wife years ago and who was supposed to die any time between his 107 and 232 years. When a character in a story continues to be alive beyond the normal length of life, it appears fantastic. But the author's intention is clear: he satirizes the patriarchal rule the cruel nature of which remains the same in the tenure of each patriarch. Marquez based his fictional dictator on a variety of real-life autocrats including Gustavo Royas Pinilla of Colombia, Generallssimo Francisco Franco of Spain and Venezuela's Juen Vicento Gomez. The rule of all these dictators, who may be different from one another in many ways, remains basically the same, revealing the disastrous effect of the concentration of power. The unnamed patriarch in the novella thus represents inhuman dictatorship in any part of the world. The author's hatred at dictatorship is revealed in his imaginary description that the news of the Patriarch's death became public not through any news agency but through the hovering of vultures over the palace. To quote the first sentence of the novel: "Over the weekend the vultures got into the Presidential Palace by pecking through the screens on the balcony windows, and the flapping of their wings stirred up the stagnant time inside, and at dawn on Monday the city awoke out of its lethargy of centuries with the warm, soft breeze of a great man dead and rotting grandeur." The story is narrated in first person plural (we) and the narrators want to be happy with the news that the patriarch of *Casa de Poder* is no more, but they cannot be sure whether the deceased is the real patriarch or his dummy. Written in long paragraphs and extended sentences, the novella is divided into six sections which do not offer any linear description but harp on the same topic—the unnamed dictator's misrule and his solitude.

Though this patriarch was an illegitimate child himself and he had begotten numerous illegitimate issues, the legitimate one born in his seventh month and conceived by his wife Leticia inherited power. The novel is full of such ironic remarks as well as fantastic descriptions such as the patriarch's having third set of original teeth at the age of one hundred and fifty. The writer's intention to satirize dictatorship is not however blurred with the use of fantasy. The sharpness of satire is rather increased with the use of grotesque elements. The patriarch in this novella provides the mass not only with oppression and poverty but also with festivals of poetry reading and beauty contest. The ruler confronted the "most terrible risks of power," laying foundation stone where the second stone was never to be laid; he had to bear up "so many soft-boiled dreams and so many repressed sighs" as he could not touch all those ephemeral and unattainable beauty queens whom he crowned; for, as he said, he had exchanged his life for the life time job of official impostor with a nominal salary of fifty pesos a month and the advantage of living like a king. The apparently innocent description of the ruler's "living like a king" scattered throughout the narrative exposes the truth of a lavish life style through satire and humor. The author also highlights the agony of solitude from which a dictator is bound to suffer. For, he cannot go out breaking the security, as his life has always been in threat and he cannot open his heart to anybody for fear of rebellion and assassination. As such a dictator has to be alert for remaining in power for life, he has to keep dummies for public appearance and such dummies often face death as they are mistaken for the ruler. Patricio Aragones, the perfect double of the unnamed ruler—he became the man most essential to the seat of power, and yet, despite his dog-like loyalty, the most feared also—was killed and nobody could know what had happened in actuality. His dead body was found by the sweeper maid next morning in his office room and it was told that his death was natural.

The dictator maintained distance from others, particularly common men and women, who were habituated to place the dictator by the side of the Almighty and adore him accordingly. One Sunday many years ago they had brought him the blind man on the street who for five coins recited the verses of the forgotten poet Rubin Darco. Though happy, the blind man could not see him, "not because he was blind but because no mortal had ever seen him since the days of the black vomit." The author uses his favorite method of exaggeration in describing how the common men including the lepers, the crippled and the blind as well as the lettered politicians and dauntless adulators proclaimed the dictator to be the corrector of earthquakes, eclipses, leap years and other errors of God. As the ruler had not been seen by the public for many years, General Roderigo arranged an open ride so that the patriots of the nation could see him in full length. The reaction of the public as rendered by the narrator is full of irony. As the ruler rode along the deserted villages of his native barren uplands, he found people waiting for him with their hands "playing mournful music, tolling death knells, displaying sign of welcome" for the nameless patriarch who set at the right hand of the Holy Trinity. Rustics from the back came to meet him in "funeral shadows of the presidential coach," and those who managed to go close enough saw only the quivering lips and the palm of a hand with no origin but waving "from the limbo of glory." The grotesque use of "playing mournful music" in welcome song adds to the queer effect of the narrative that sketches the dictator in a subversive way. It is suggested that the ruler actually deserved funeral song after so many years of survival. The shameless greed of the politicians who are always hankering for power is however exposed in an unambiguous way. It was stated that the dictator had died of natural causes during his sleep, but the high command was delaying the notice while they tried to "settle in bloody secret meetings their postponed quarrels." It was also stated that the Liberals who had sold the Federalist war, the conservatives who had bought it, the generals of the high command, three cabinet ministers, the archbishop all together in one single plot calling for the "unity of all against the despotism of center" so that they could divide up among themselves the "booty of his death so absorbed in the depths of greed that no one noticed the appearance of the unburied president." At last a coffin with gold trim and purple ribbons for the dead body of the president was brought in a military van, and still the narrator seemed to be afraid of the ruler's reappearance with authoritarian rule, for, as the concluding line says, "we knew that no evidence of his death was final, because there was always another truth behind the truth." The author's fear that the death of a particular dictator is not the proof of the removal of dictatorship altogether is revealed here. His first hand knowledge of the continuous rule of oppression in Latin America and particularly in the states of the Caribbean coast and his desperate attempt to reveal the picture of that oppression in fiction resulted in this wonderful creation.[5]

The present chapter, 'History, Mundane Reality and Fantasy in Marquez's Fiction,' tries to focus on Marquez's peculiar practice of amalgamating history, contemporary political condition and fantasy together in his fictional writings. His narrative mode as well as the proportion of these different materials to be blended in his writing varies from fiction to fiction. In *One Hundred Years of Solitude* he draws liberally from the history of Colombia and the past of the continent at large, from its discovery by the Europeans to colonial times and the war of independence. And the entire novel is narrated in a style that obliterates the difference between dream and reality, myth and history while representing a world of cultural merger without condescending to it as primitive but showing it as deprived. *In Evil Hour* depicts the contemporary history through projection of a wretched land where nothing changes except governments and the voice of opposition is mercilessly crushed. The narrative mode is different from that of *One Hundred Years of Solitude* and the writer takes up an ironic mode having imaginative richness and easy accessibility, filled up with satire and humor through exaggerated details. *No One Writes to the Colonel* with its universal appeal is almost free from any fantasy while *The Autumn of the Patriarch,* with its unusually long sentences used to reveal the loneliness and atrocities of a dictator who lives through out many generations and thereby breaks the rules of the real world, generates a feeling of suffocation. Though the phrase 'magic realism'[6] is frequently used in Marquez criticism the phrase is insufficient while analyzing the art of Marquez that varies widely. Marquez also said many times that in his fiction he concentrated on reality and had little to do with fantasy, though he had to choose different styles according to the demand of his theme. As he said in an interview, "One does not choose the style. . . . But the style is determined by the subject, by the mood of the time. If you try to use something that is not suitable, it just won't work. Then the critics build theories around that and they see things I hadn't seen. I only respond to our way of life, the life of the Caribbean."[7] As the definitions of 'magic realism' offered by different critics do not give full justice to the fictional writings of Marquez, several critics attempt alternative understanding of Marquez's art. To quote Michael Bell in this context, "what is really at stake is a psychological suppleness which is able to inhabit unsentimentally the daytime world while remaining open to the promptings of those domains which modern culture has, by its own inner logic, necessarily marginalized or repressed"[8]. In Marquez's fiction, the line of demarcation between the "daytime world," that is the mundane world that we feel with our five senses in broad daylight, and the world of our dream or imagination that usually overpower us in darkness or in twilight, is blurred. Marquez's preference is obviously, the daytime world, and the fantasy is used as a technique or mode of narration as per the demand of the story based on mundane reality.

Notes

1 Though the issues taken up by Marquez for his fiction emerged from the specific problems of his own country Colombia, they were also the socio-political-cultural issues that confronted the Latin American continent. Marquez's intention was to change the outlook of the people in general whose cultural orientation compelled them to see the world through Anglo Saxon eyes. Christopher Columbus's 'discovery' of America in 1492 initiated a long chain of unfortunate events. The 'discovery' released the Renaissance imagination itself. The reports of Amerigo Vespucci, the Italian navigator, encouraged Sir Thomas More to invent an ideal society in 'Utopia' (1515). Roger Bacon claimed that three mechanical inventions—printing, gunpowder and magnet—changed the whole face and state of things throughout the world. The immensely rich cultures of the Mayas, the Aztecs and the Incas having been systematically obliterated, the possible

flowering of an authentic American civilization was nipped in the bud. In some countries of Latin America these rich civilizations were uprooted completely while in others the native Indians were banished to the remote country side, far away from the urban centers of power and were reduced to a marginal existence. Colonial rule in Latin America created a vacuum that gave way to the unequal encounter of three different races that had never met each other before: the European white, the Indigenous Indian and the African black. The encounter of the three races is imbued with such deep significance that the Cuban novelist Alejo Carpentier considered the 'discovery' to be the most important watershed in history, alienating the New World Man from the Pre-Colombian man. Crisis of identity and search for an authentic form thus became an abiding concern of all the Latin American artists. Neruda's invocation of 'The Heights of Macchu Picchu' or Vallejo's lamentation in 'Trilce' are moments when personal anguish moves to a broader vision of suffering humanity.

2 No eminent Latin American author of mid twentieth century was attracted towards the pursuit of a self-referential inward-looking art. For them life and art were too closely bound up, the experience of reality too urgent to be ignored. A new social situation defines the position of the artist, who then finds a technique to suit his/her purpose.

3 Although coffee is generally considered Colombia's main export, banana was also of crucial importance to the country's economy. During the first few decades of the twentieth century, the United Fruit Company, an American outfit, had a virtual monopoly over the banana industry which at that time was the only source of income for many people in the coastal area. The United Fruit Company enjoyed unlimited economic power and tremendous political clout, and was a corrupt and amoral company that exploited its Colombian workers terribly. In October of 1928, over twenty thousand native workers went on strike, demanding among other things, hygienic working conditions, medical treatment, functioning toilets and payments in cash. Although the native laborers worked seven days a week, they were denied the status of employee and were therefore exempted from Colombian labor laws and safety regulations. There were repeated strikes as the company ignored the demands, and soon the Colombian

government occupied the banana zone and employed the military to tackle the laborers on strike. One night in December, a huge crowd gathered in Cienaga, thirty miles north of Arcataca, to hold a demonstration. The conservative government sent the troops who fired on the workers, killing hundreds; and finally, the whole incident was officially denied and struck off the record.

4 One of the most horrible episodes in Colombian history, known as *la violencia,* had its root in the massacre of the American Fruit Company. At that time Jorge Eliecer Gaitan, a young Liberal member of Congress had the courage to take stand against the government corruption and he convened meetings to investigate the incident. Gradually Gaitan became a champion of the poor and the peasants. But he was strongly opposed by the powerful members of both the parties who feared him and also loathed him. He continued campaigning for true democracy and heralded a time of change. By 1946 he was powerful enough to cause a split in Liberal party which had been in power in since 1930. The split caused a Conservative return to power and this government with its loud propaganda of bringing democracy in the land organized parliamentary groups whose ultimate intention was to terrorize Liberal voters. There were innumerable killings in ambush and the country suffered from continuous riots and bloodshed. In 1947, under the leadership of Gaitar, the Liberals gained control of the Congress. But the situation worsened as Gaitar was assassinated on April 9, 1948, in Bogota. The city was convulsed by lethal riots for three days, a period called *el Bogotazo,* and 2500 lives were killed in those three days. *La violencia* entered a more deadly phase with both the parties organizing guerilla armies. Towns and villages were burned, thousands of people including women and children were brutally killed and millions of peasants escaped to Venezuela. In 1949, one Liberal leader was gunned down while giving a speech in the Congress Hall. The country was declared to be in a state of siege and the reign of horror continued. *La violencia* is said to have claimed about 200000 people by 1953.

5 About *The Autumn of the Patriarch* Marquez said, "My intention was always to make a synthesis of all the Latin American dictators but especially those from the Caribbean. Nevertheless, the personality of Juan Vicanto Gomez (of Venezuela) was so strong in addition to the fact that he exercised a special fascination over

me, that undoubtedly the patriarch has much more of him than anyone else." Quoted in Raymond L. Williams' *Gabriel Garcia Marquez* ,(1984; Boston; Twayne Publishers), p.112

6 The phrase 'magic realism' was first used by the German art critic Franz Roh in 1925 to refer to a style in painting which is also known as the New Objectivity. Roh believed that 'magic realism' is related to but distinct from 'surrealism' which explores the more cerebral, psychological and subconscious reality. 'Magic realism' was later used to describe the uncanny realism by painters like Ivan Albright, Paul Cadmus and other artists during the 1940s and 50s. It does not often include overtly fantastic or magical content, but rather looks at the mundane reality through a hyper-realistic and often mysterious lens. There are differences of opinion in regard to its use in literary criticism. But most of the critics argue that 'Magic Realism'(in Spanish, *el realism magical*), came to be used in the field of literary criticism for the first time in 1949 by the Cuban novelist Alejo Carpentier to describe the matter-of-fact combination of the fantastic and the everyday life in Latin American fiction. About the same time the term was also used by the European critics to describe a similar trend in postwar German fiction exemplified by novel like Gunter Grass's *The Tin Drum* (1959). Magic Realism has now become the standard name for a major trend in contemporary fiction that opposes the twentieth century Realistic novel of Europe as it expands the categories of the real so as to encompass myth, magic and other extraordinary experiences which European Realism excluded. To quote J.A. Cuddon's definition of Magic Realism, "A magical realist text betrays features like cultural hybridity, mixing western empirical-realist mode with the eastern mythological one. Also there could be skilful time shifts, convoluted and even labyrinthine narratives and plots, miscellaneous use of dreams, myths and fairy stories, expressionistic and even surrealistic description, arcane erudition , the element of surprise or abrupt shock, the horrific and the inexplicable" (*A Dictionary of Literary Terms*).

7 Simons Marlise: 'Gabriel Marquez on Love, Plague and Politics,' *The New York Times, 21 Feb.*1988. Retrieved 30 July, 2008..

8 Bell, Michael: *Gabriel Garcia Marquez: Solitude and Solidarity* (1993; Hampshire; Macmillan), p.49.

Solitude, Solidarity and Love in Marquez's Fiction

Solitude is a strong motif in Marquez's fictional writings and generally speaking, his fiction often reveals a search for a way out of solitude. Marquez interpreted the colonial rules in Latin America and its aftermath—the long time of seclusion from the outer world and also of the world of science—as time of solitude, opposed to the time of solidarity. His celebrated novel *One Hundred Years of Solitude* and his Nobel Prize acceptance speech 'The Solitude of Latin America,' with their political overtone attached to the word 'solitude,' harp on the sufferings attached to solitude that had been imposed on the Latin American countries. In his other writings too, solitude is projected as an almost inescapable condition. In his Nobel Prize acceptance speech Marquez directly attacks the dominant European and North American powers for treating the Latin Americans as culturally 'other,' and hence inferior to them, since the days of the 'discovery' of Latin America by the outsiders. Having described the plight of the forced exiles of Latin America—those exiles outnumber the total population of Norway, he claimed—Marquez observed that the agony of countless daily deaths in the continent nourished a source of insatiable creativity drawing the attention of the Swedish Academy. To quote the words from his address, "Poets and beggars, musicians and prophets, warriors and scoundrels, all creatures of that unbridled reality, we have had to ask but little of imagination, for our crucial problem has been a lack of conventional means to render our lives believable. This, my friends, is the crux of our solitude"[1] (*www.nobelprize.org./*

nobel_prizes/literatures/1982/marquez-lecture. html.) This inability to render one's agony believable is the cause of solitude both at national level and at personal level. The nature of solitude felt by all the Latin American countries in general is clarified in Marquez's Nobel Prize acceptance speech while the nature of solitude at personal level is rendered through the portrayal of characters in his fictional writings.

Marquez attributes the solitude felt at national level to colonial legacies. Thanks to their insistence on measuring the Latin American culture and civilization with "the yardstick that they use for themselves," the dominant European nations found the Latin American culture uncivilized and inferior, and therefore, no real communication with them was ever possible. Marquez complained, "The interpretation of our reality through patterns not our own serves only to make us even more unknown, even less free, even more solitary" (Nobel Prize Address). Moreover, political interferences of the powerful states into the domestic affairs of the Latin American countries are at the root of blood sheds and atrocities going on in these countries. Political unrest also gave birth to horrifying social problems. As Marquez told in his speech, during the postcolonial period there were five wars and seventeen military coups in which numerous women were arrested while pregnant and they gave birth in prisons. But nobody knows the whereabouts and the identity of those children who were furtively adopted or sent to orphanage by order of the military authorities. As the atrocities caused by the military rulers, powerful with the support from the foreign countries, started the process of weakening ties between culture and space, the land became more and more secluded from its own past and from the world outside. Marquez raised the question of social equality in an unequivocal tone: "Why think that the social justice sought by progressive Europeans for their own countries cannot also be a goal for Latin America with its different methods for dissimilar conditions? No: the immeasurable violence and pain of our history are the result of age-old inequalities and untold bitterness, and not a conspiracy plotted three thousand leagues from our home. But many European leaders and thinkers have thought so . . . as if it were impossible to find another destiny than to live at the mercy of the two great masters of the world. This, my friends, is the very scale of our solitude" (Nobel Prize Address). To get an escape from the agony of such solitude Marquez recommended solidarity with powerful foreign powers, but he apprehended that his suggested solidarity would not be possible in reality: "Solidarity with our dreams will not make us less alone, as long as it is not translated into concrete acts or legitimate support for all the peoples that assume the illusion of having a life of their own, in the distribution of the world" (Nobel Prize Address). Solitude at national level, as Marquez conceived of it, might be removed through exercises of true freedom which is opposed to any illusory vision. The Nobel lecture ends with an optimistic observation that solitude had not stood on the way of their responding with life in a positive way. The author hopes of creating a new utopia "where no one will be able to decide for others how they die, where love will prove true. . .and where the races condemned to one hundred years of solitude will have at last and forever, a second opportunity on earth" (Nobel Prize Address).

One Hundred Years of Solitude begins with a search of its founder Jose Arcadio Buendia to get out of the solitude of Macondo the village he established along with his companions a few years ago. The village was in fact lost in the drowsiness of the swamp with little or no connection with the world outside. Since the arrival of the gypsies, however, who brought with them 'marvelous' objects for sale and more marvelous stories about the scientific inventions in far away land, a sort of faint connection with the outer world was visible. But a man like Jose Arcadio Buendia felt more secluded than ever and was attacked by the fever of "the magnets, the astronomical calculations, dreams of transmutation, and the urge to discover the wonders of the world" (15-16). He felt sorry that his choice of Macondo as a place for settlement had not been prudent and so he started once again the tedious adventure along with his faithful attendants "to open a way that would put Macondo in contact with the great inventions" (16). Completely ignorant of the geography of the region, Jose Arcadio Buenda calculated that the only possibility of contact with civilization lay with the northern route and he undertook the reckless adventure towards the north. For a week, almost without speaking, they went ahead like sleepwalkers "through a universe of grief, lighted only by the tenuous reflection of luminous insects" (17), and Jose Arcadio Buendia, always following his compass, kept on guiding his men "toward the invisible north" in order to get out of that enchanted region. One morning they found an enormous Spanish galleon with its intact masts and dirty rags of its sails, the whole structure occupying its own space, "one of solitude and oblivion, protected from the vices of time." The discovery of the galleon, an indication of the proximity of the sea, filled their mind with the hope of finding a sea route. But when after a journey of four days, they found the ashen, foamy, dirty sea, Jose Arcadio Buendia was disheartened that the dirty sea did not merit the risks and sacrifices of the adventure and his hopes to make an end of solitude were belied. He lamented to Ursula that they had been stuck to a land that would continue to be deprived of the benefits of science and he made another plan to leave that place on his own as nobody in the village was ready to follow him any-more. This time Ursula disposed the plan and eventually Jose Arcadio Buendia's utter solitude led him towards insanity. His loss of memory was also caused by his solitude which was obviously lessened by Melquiades, the first gypsy in Macondo, who had been out of touch for many years and who came again when he was most needed. He had really been through death and he returned because "he could not bear the solitude." "Repudiated by his tribe, having lost all of his supernatural faculties because of his faithfulness to life, he decided to take refuge in that corner of the world which had still not been discovered by death, dedicated to the operation of a daguerreotype laboratory" (47). But Melquiades could not remove the utter loneliness of Jose Arcadio Buendia who represented the solitude of Macondo. At first Jose Arcadio Buendia helped Melquiades in his work, enthusiastic over the novelty of photograph and the predictions of Nostradamus. "But little by little he began abandoning him to his solitude, for communication was becoming increasingly difficult" (65). After his solitude took him beyond this mundane world and he could never come back to reality, he was tied to a chestnut tree in the courtyard. He remained there for years in total seclusion, his mind not responding to the grave tragedies faced by his family.

Other characters in this novel who suffer from pangs of solitude are not sketched with such massive background as is done in Jose Arcadio Buendia's case. Colonel Aureliano Buendia is however different from others, both in his attitude to love and his performance in war. His experience of sex with the adolescent mulatto girl when he felt "terribly alone," the death of his young wife Remedios that created in him "a solitary and passive frustration similar to the one he had felt during the time he was resigned to living without women" (84), his countless encounters during war when he felt terribly secluded from time and space and the solitude attached to his immense power as a leader of people render him as an extraordinary person whose suffering from solitude was also extraordinary. Marquez summarized the extraordinary events of his life in a few sentences. "Colonel Aureliano Buendia organized thirty two armed uprisings and he lost them all. He had seventeen male children by seventeen different and they were exterminated one after the other on a single night before the oldest one had reached the age of thirty-five. He survived fourteen attempts on his life, seventy-three ambushes, and a firing squad. He lived through a dose of strychnine in his coffee that was enough to kill a horse. He refused the Order of Merit, which the President of the Republic awarded him. He rose to be Commander-in-Chief of the revolutionary forces, with jurisdiction and command from one border to the other, and the man most feared by the government, but he never let himself be photographed" (91). Surprisingly, however, he was a very sensitive man in his youth, seriously engaged in his work in laboratory or in writing poems. Both the activities badly needed self-absorption and therefore he voluntarily accepted a solitary condition. A man capable of taking full responsibility of his action, Aureliano Buendia always chose for himself a quality that needed seclusion: when he wanted to marry Remedios, the youngest daughter of the mayor of the town who was not in the good book of his father—and he even waited for a long period of time till she became matured—he took the decision all alone. After the untimely death of his wife he would meet his father-in-law regularly not intending to marry one of his five daughters who were still unmarried, but because he was driven by a sense of void arising out of his solitude. During the time he played dominoes with his father-in-law, he came in contact with political activities of the time and leaned towards the Liberal party; but hardly did he feel solidarity with other members of the party. That time the rebel in the guise of a doctor was staying in Macondo who made contact with the young people of the town, inspiring them with his faith in violence. "The majority of Aureliano's friends were enthusiastic over the idea of liquidating the Conservative government, but no one had dared include him in the plans, not only because of his ties with the magistrate, but because of his solitary and elusive character" (87). Because of this nature Aureliano did not hesitate to call the doctor a butcher when he called on him. Basically a humanist, Aureliano raised his voice against murder. But after he was aware of the brutal killing of the doctor without due process of law and of other massacres by the Conservative government, his hesitation for bloodshed was gone forever. From this time on, Colonel Aureliano Buendia's sense of solitude began to increase alarmingly, as he was now secluded not only from the outer world but also from his own real self. He stopped writing poetry and never went inside the laboratory during his stay at home in between the wars. For Marquez, war and bloodshed are opposed to love which alone can remove solitude, and this love needs to be differentiated from passion which hardly leaves a mark on one's mind. Thus his occasional sex relationships could never lessen the pangs of his solitude. Everybody including Ursula got surprised and even stupefied when he came to his house in Macondo without any escort and wrapped in a cloak in spite of the heat, and with three mistresses, whom he installed in the same house, where he spent most of his time lying in a hammock. "He had not returned to reading his poetry, which filled more than five volumes and lay forgotten at the bottom of his trunk. At night or at siesta time he would call one of his women to his hammock and obtain a rudimentary satisfaction from her, and then he would sleep like a stone that was not concerned by the slightest indication of worry" (138). It is a picture of perfect seclusion from one's own self as well as the world outside. This time he decided that no human being, not even Ursula, could come closer to him than ten feet. In the center of the chalk circle drawn by his aides wherever he stopped, only he could enter to give brief orders.

Marquez offered a close study of solitude attached to rising power through the portrait of Colonel Aureliano Buendia. When his authority was recognized by all the rebel commanders, he was shaken by a latent fear which automatically becomes part and parcel of absolute power. He could not sleep well, often waking up in a fright, calling for a blanket. An inner coldness that shattered his bones and tortured him even in the heat of the sun would not let him sleep for several months, until it became a habit. The intoxication of power began to break apart under waves of discomfort. Searching for a cure against the chill, he had the young officer, who had proposed the murder of General Teofilo Vargas, shot. The author said, rather ironically, that his orders were being carried out even before they were given, even before he thought of them, and they always went much beyond what he would have dared have them do. Here is a realistic study of the activities of a group of over-enthusiastic and over-active supporters who always surround the centre of power and the person who is in power, intoxicated and secluded from the mass, having lost all sense of decency and morality. To quote Marquez, "Lost in solitude of his immense power, he (Aureliano) began to lose direction. He was bothered by the people who cheered him in neighboring villages, and he imagined that they were the same cheers they gave the enemy. Everywhere he met adolescents who looked at him with his own eyes, who spoke to him with his own voice, and greeted him with the same mistrust with which he greeted them, and who said they were his sons. He felt scattered about, multiplied, and more solitary than ever" (140). A loss of faith in others, doubt in everything and a secret sense of fear of loosing power are revealed in the paragraph quoted above. This is a picture of utter loneliness from which a leader—he may be an autocratic ruler of the country or an opposition leader having absolute power in his party—is destined to suffer. In *Autumn of the Patriarch,* Marquez rendered the picture of solitude to which a ruling dictator is condemned. While a ruling dictator has an easy luxurious life at hand, a rebel like Colonel Aureliano Buendia has to suffer physical agony; but in both the cases when they enjoy absolute power, they have to remain in solitude. This solitude cannot be removed through physical contact and so his sex relationship had no effect on his mind. It was neither love nor passion but the custom of sending virgins to the bedrooms of the soldiers that was the cause behind the birth of his seventeen sons. All these sons were brought home to be baptized after a few years of their birth and all of them, destined to suffer from solitude, were killed in ambush after they joined the war. Ursula, who had not known earlier of this custom, was naturally taken aback when they brought children of all ages and all colors but with a look of solitude that left no doubt as to the relation. The word 'solitude,' used in connection with Aureliano's sons (who are to be called bastards or at least illegitimate, as per the civilized Western standards) carries social implications. Aureliano is thus projected not only as a person who suffered immensely from solitude, but also as a man who had begotten a generation of men, all affected by solitude. His acute consciousness and capacity of self-analysis attached to his sense of solitude made him a complex character. Such picture of solitude is pathetic as when Aureliano, "alone, abandoned by his premonitions, fleeing the chill that was to accompany him until death, he sought a last refuge in Macondo in the warmth of his oldest memories" (140). His self realization that he was fighting only for power aggravated his suffering from solitude. After twenty years of war, having acquired the aura of legend that glowed about his presence, he was changed into a stranger in his town. In his house he was so much merged in himself that he hardly noticed others in the family. Not only the present, but also the past was wiped out of his mind. Even his wife Remedois became a hazy image of someone else. The countless women he had known in "the desert of love and who had spread his seed all along the coast" had left no trace in his feelings. During the days preceding the one fixed for armistice, his frustration led him to destroy all those things which had traces of him. When he wanted to destroy the photograph of Remedois, he was prevented from doing so by Ursula who proclaimed that the picture had ceased to belong to him and became a family relic which he could not destroy. Having destroyed all the objects in the house that would let him be remembered, he took the trunk of poetry to the bakery to burn the roll of papers. Not only did he burn the papers but also broke the trunk up with a hatchet and threw the pieces in fire. When his personal physician came for the treatment of his sores, he asked the doctor, without showing any particular interest where the exact location of his heart was. The doctor examined his chest with his stethoscope and then painted a circle on his chest with a piece of cotton dipped in iodine. On the day of the armistice, when Colonel Marquez came to fetch him, he found Aureliano "more taciturn than ever, more pensive and solitary." After signing the documents, Aureliano went to take rest in a tent prepared for him and then shot himself in the iodine circle painted by the physician. Thanks to the doctor, who had apprehended the Colonel's suicidal tendency and misled him, he survived. The failure of his death brought back his lost prestige. When he recovered after two months, he decided not to think of war again and devoted him to his workshop, preparing little gold fishes. Gradually he lost contact with the reality of the nation. Enclosed in his workshop, his only contact with the outer world was his business in little gold fishes. In fact, it was not the business but work itself that interested him. He needed so much concentration to link scales, fit minute rubies into the eyes, laminate gills, and put on fins that there was not the smallest empty moment left for him to fill with his disillusionment with the war. Though because of his absorbed attention in the work he was soon aged, the implacable concentration awarded him with a peace of mind. Thus he passed through different phases of solitude and towards the end of his life realized that "the secret of a good old age is simply an honorable pact with solitude" (166).

Other characters in the novel also encounter solitude in their own ways. With a unique strength of mind and body, Ursula had accompanied her husband in the adventurous journey across the hills to get at a new settlement, went out of home alone chasing the gypsies in search of her eldest son and came back with some of the gypsies who settled in Macondo, controlled her highly imaginative husband who went crazy, and besides looking after the increasing members of her family she interfered into public matters, and yet, maybe for performing those herculean tasks all alone, she felt terribly secluded. For example, after the mayor Don Apolinar Moscote had been dragged out of his home, his furniture destroyed and his daughters flogged by the Liberal party members, Ursula controlled the rebels in strong hand and in a way ruled the town, reestablishing the Sunday mass and abrogating the harebrained decrees, and yet "she felt so much alone that she sought the useless company of her husband, who had been forgotten under the chestnut tree" (93). Again, the moment Colonel Aureliano Buendia shot himself, Ursula, who was in Macondo far away from the place where the treaty was signed, found the pot of milk full of worms and guessed that Aureliano must have been shot. She found no living soul to console her in utter distress and had no other way but to look toward the courtyard where her husband had been tied to a tree, obeying a habit of solitude. And then she saw Jose Arcadio Buendia, soaking wet and sad in the rain and much older than when he had died. 'They shot him in the back,' Ursula said more precisely, 'and no one was charitable enough to close his eyes.' The agony of a lonely mother apprehending the death of her dearest son could hardly be better described. At dusk through her tears she saw the swift and luminous discs that crossed the sky like an exhalation and the thought that it was a signal of death. She was still under the chestnut tree, sobbing at her husband's knees, when they brought in Colonel Aureliano Buendia, "wrapped in a blanket that was stiff with dry blood and with his eyes open in rage" (149). When she saw that her son was going to live, she resumed her usual duties. Even when she was already a hundred years old and on the point of going blind from cataracts, she still had her physical dynamism, her integrity of character, and her mental balance intact. She analyzed the causes behind the downfall of their line and categorized them as enthusiasm for war, fighting cocks, relationship with bad women and wild undertakings. Vexed with the vices of the members of her family, she had not yet lost hope and declared that she would bring up the new born first son of Aureliano Segundo, keeping him away from all those vices so that he would become Pope in future. A character sketched in epic style, Ursula, too in her last days, was immersed in memories and thus made an honorable pact with solitude.

Pietro Crespi, the Italian, "whose head covered with patent leather curls aroused in women an irrepressible need to sigh" (67), is quite a different type of character who was lacking in mental strength and whose suffering from solitude arising out of his frustration from disappointment in love led him to commit suicide. It is possible that Marquez intended to sketch the Italian as quite a different person, having little similarities with the Caribbean. With the use of subtle irony he sketched the character as sentimental, opposed to the manliness of the Caribbean people, to point at the basic differences between the two races. Thus Pietro Crespi could think of committing suicide having been disappointed in love, and this very act shows the racial difference between a European and a Caribbean as the latter can hardly be imagined as a frustrated lover committing suicide. Anyway, this Italian set up a store for musical instruments and mechanical toys in the same section of Macondo where the Arabs had lingered in other times swapping knick-knacks for macaws, and which the people called the Street of the Turks. First, he fell in love with Rebeca and even formalized his promise to her. But Amaranta also fell in love with him and Pietro Crespi dealt with her as with a capricious little girl who was not worth talking seriously. Amaranta felt humiliated and told him with a virulent anger that she was prepared to stop his marriage with Rebeca even at the cost of her life. The marriage was not held on the scheduled day as Crespi received a telegram of his mother's serious condition which was found false. Because of Remedios's sudden death the date of the marriage could not be fixed. In the meantime Jose Arcadio's passion for Rebeca became so strong that he married her almost forcibly. As Pietro Crespi was affectionately treated by Ursula, he continued having lunch in the house on Tuesdays, rising above his defeat with a serene dignity. Amaranta looked after him with "a loving diligence" and he too found that whom he had treated as a child was a revelation. The two "deepened their friendship" and enjoyed Ursula's support. "It was a twilight engagement. The Italian would arrive at dusk, with a gardenia in his buttonhole, and he would translate Petrarch's sonnets for Amaranta. They would sit on the porch, suffocated by the oregano and the roses, he reading and she sewing lace cuffs." (94). Pietro Crespi felt that after crossing the ocean in search of love, after "having confused passion with the vehement stroking of Rebeca," he at last found it in Amaranta. Everybody in the town felt that they would be a good match. When Ursula ordered the revival of Sunday mass, Pietro Crespi donated a German harmonium to the church, organized a children's chorus and prepared a Gregorian repertory. "No one doubted that he would make Amaranta a fortunate mate" (95). But Amaranta's strong refusal was heart-breaking and he lost control of himself. "He wept shamelessly, almost breaking his fingers with desperation, but he could not break her down . . . He went through incredible extremes of humiliation. He wept one whole afternoon in Ursula's lap and she would have sold her soul in order to comfort him" (95). His mourning for his frustrated love continued for months together and at last, on second November, All Souls' Day, his brother found him dead inside the shop, amidst all the lighted lamps, all the music boxes open and all the clocks striking in interminable hour. It was found that he had cut his wrists by a razor. Pietro Crespi's love was platonic; any physical relationship either with Rebeca or with Amaranta has not been suggested in the novel.

His suicide may be interpreted as romantic excess, an act of foolhardiness that has little to do with real life. And the solitude from which he suffered was also a romantic feeling of loneliness, hardly related to reality.

Rebeca, who did not belong to the Buendia family but took shelter there as an orphan, is rendered as psychologically weak and naturally, she could not tackle solitude in an intelligent way. She suffered the pangs of solitude in her own way when Amaranta threatened her or when her marriage with Pietro Crespi was postponed. Amaranta was not only very shrewd and calculative, but also keen on taking vengeance. To take revenge on Pietro Crespi, who did not reciprocate her feelings and treated her as a child, she left no stone unturned. That it was her vicious plan to postpone his marriage with Rebeca is clearly hinted in the novel. The cause behind Remedios's sudden and mysterious death is not revealed, but there is no doubt that her death put a hurdle on the proposed marriage much to Amaranta's satisfaction. She was also the cause behind the suicide of Pietro Crespi. Having accompanied him for a long time and having created an atmosphere that led everyone to believe that she was going to marry the Italian, she did not agree to marry him, exposing her sadistic nature. Her suffering from "the barb of a lonely love" after she discovered Rebeca's passion originated from jealousy and such a person is destined to suffer for her own nature. Lastly, Colonel Gerineldo Marquez who also loved Amaranta sincerely for many years was rebuffed by her. When he became gradually disinterested in war and took refuge in her sewing room, they spent many hours together without speaking and he was happy in her company. Amaranta was inwardly pleased in keeping the fire of his devotion alive, but he was "unaware of the secret design of that indecipherable heart" (136). Even during the most critical days of the war he visited her every afternoon and many times even turned the wheel of her sewing machine. Amaranta felt upset by the perseverance, the loyalty, the submissiveness of that man who was invested with so much authority. For four years he kept repeating his love and she would always find a way to reject him without hurting him, "for even though she had not succeeded in loving him she could no longer live without him" (137). Amaranta suddenly discovered that the girl Remedios the Beauty whom she had brought up had become the most beautiful girl in the region. "She felt reborn in her heart the rancor that she had felt in other days for Rebeca, and begging God not to impel her into the extreme state of wishing her dead, she banished her from the sewing room" (137). It was by that time that Colonel Marquez was ready to give up for Amaranta a glory that had cost him the sacrifice of his best years. But he could not succeed in convincing her. "One August afternoon, overcome by the unbearable weight of her own obstinacy, Amaranta locked herself in her bedroom to weep over her solitude unto death after giving her final answer to her tenacious suitor" (137). That afternoon Colonel Marquez also "looked at the desolate streets, the crystal water on the almond trees, and he found himself lost in solitude" (138). Thus *One Hundred Years of Solitude* is a wonderful reading from the aspect of a study of solitude. While Macondo is the symbol of solitude of Latin America, most of the important characters in the novel embrace solitude in their respective ways.

Another significant rendering of solitude and love is found in *Chronicle of a Death Foretold,* a novella which is apparently a collection of data from the witnesses to reconstruct a murder that had occurred twenty seven years before. It was an honor killing done by two brothers of a bride Angela Vicario, who was returned by her husband on the wedding night for her failure to show proof of her virginity. Pressurized by her brothers Angela had to utter the name of a local Arab young man Santiago Nasar—it is clearly suggested however that Angela had not been seduced by anybody—who was killed in brought day light and Angela was punished with a secluded life. It is significant that though Angela did not want to marry Bayardo San Roman as she had cherished the desire of marrying someone whom she could love and therefore preferred to wait for the advent of an overwhelming passion in her mind, she had to succumb to her family's decisive argument that "a family dignified by modest means had no right to disdain that prize of destiny." Her mother's single phrase that love can be learned too, demolished all her arguments for the inconvenience of lack of love. Ironically, Angela was blessed with that overwhelming passion for which she had been waiting at a totally unexpected time, and that too, for her husband who returned her. To quote the narrator's interview with Angela: "Bayardo San Roman had been in her life forever from the moment he'd brought her back home. It was a coup de grace. 'Suddenly, when Mama began to hit me, I began to remember him,' she told me. The blows hurt less because she knew they were for him. She continued thinking about him with a certain surprise at herself while she was lying on the dining room coach sobbing. 'I wasn't crying because of the blows or anything that had happened,' she told me, 'I was crying because of him'" (92). From that moment on her new found love accompanied her through the days of utter humiliation and solitude, to which she was thrown after bringing the dishonor to her parent's family. "She was reborn," the narrator informs. She had the opportunity to see Bayardo San Roman from afar only once after she was returned. This incident made her crazy and from now on she had only to close her eyes to see him. Unable to a get a moment's rest she began to write to him, one letter per month, all without reply. Living the life of a rejected wife in seclusion and continuing the work of embroidery, she also developed in the meantime an understanding of life. Her pure love, stripped of all desires, acted as a glow inside her mind. "She became lucid overbearing, mistress of her own free will, and she became a virgin again just for him, and she recognized no other authority than her own nor any other service than that of her obsession" (94)[2].

The theme of solitude and love runs through *Love in the Time of Cholera* (1985) in a more prominent way. As Ruben Pelayo observes, "*Love in the Time of Cholera*, like all of Garcia Marquez's works, explores the solitude of the individual and of human kind. . .portrayed through the solitude of love and of being in love"[3]. The setting is a postcolonial Caribbean district of La Manga, where until a few years ago some old mulattoes could be seen bearing the royal slave brand that had been burnt onto their chests. "Independence from Spain and then the abolition of slavery precipitated the conditions of honorable decadence. . . . The great old families sank into their ruined palaces in silence. Along the rough cobbled streets that had served so well in surprise attacks and buccaneer landings, weeds hung from the balconies and opened cracks in the whitewashed walls of even the best kept mansions, and the only signs of life at two o'clock in the afternoon were languid piano exercises played in the light of siesta" (17). This was the picture of the colonial city where Dr. Juvenal Urbino, one of the important characters in the novel, who was eighty one when the story begins, was born and raised. The author also refers to the historical incident that took place on Friday, June 8, 1708: the galleon *San Jose* set sail for Cadiz with a cargo of precious stones and metals valued at five hundred billion pesos in the currency of the day; it was sunk by an English squadron at the entrance to the port and two centuries later it had not yet been salvaged. The setting with its memory of the drowned ship and the corpse of the commander creates an atmosphere of loss and seclusion.

The novel starts with two deaths—one, suicide of a photographer at the age of sixty and the other, an accidental death of a renowned physician at the age of eighty one. The photographer, an Antillean refugee Jeremiah de Saint-Amor, was a disabled war veteran—he used crutches and had an old scar across his stomach—and he lived alone with a dog, his only pastime being to play chess in the evening. It is soon known that he had regular contact with a woman whom he did not marry and who was in mourning after his death. To commit suicide he consumed the cyanide vapors activated in a tray by some photographic acid as he believed that one must die with grace before one becomes old. He was a friend of Dr. Juvenal Urbino who would play chess with him during evening and who came to his residence after getting the news of the death. Because of the doctor's interference there was no autopsy and the body was directly taken for last ritual. Having seen the dead body the doctor found on the desk the chessboard with an unfinished game. Usually he always finished every game and then placed the board and chessmen in the box that was stored in a desk drawer. If there were any doubt regarding the suicide and any suspected crime, the doctor thought, the unfinished game—in which the white pieces were going to be defeated and Jeremiah always played with the white ones—could be used as a good clue. But the doctor was very sure from the beginning that it was clearly a case of suicide and hence he did not much bother about the game. While the doctor was studying the unfinished game, the inspector discovered an envelope, tightly sealed, addressed to Dr. Juvenal Urbino. The doctor opened the envelope and gave a quick glance at the eleven sheets, with agitated breath. He looked pale after the reading and his fingers trembled, but when asked about the letter's content, he replied that there was nothing in particular but his final instructions. Having organized everything about the burial that was scheduled to be held at 5 o'clock in the afternoon, the doctor consulted the letter again before undertaking a confidential visit in an obscure location in the old slave quarter. He visited a lady in her dress of mourning and understood that the lady knew more than he did about everything stated in the letter. The doctor, though he claimed to be the deceased person's friend, had not known earlier that the lady had been with him for half his life, "with a devotion and submissive tenderness that bore too close a resemblance to love, and without anyone knowing anything about it in this sleepy provincial capital where even state secrets were common knowledge" (13). It is indeed surprising that nobody had any knowledge about the relationship of the two. Dr. Urbino never could have believed that his friend had a woman if he himself had not written it in the letter. In any event it was difficult for him to comprehend why two free adults without a past and living on the fringes of a close society's prejudices had chosen the hazards of illicit love. The lady explained to the doctor that it was the wish of Jeremiah de Saint-Amour and that it was exemplary. She also gave him details of their activities on the previous night—their going to the cinema, each one separately, their meeting in his laboratory, their playing chess in which he played inattentively and surrendered without honor. Though she first thought that the brutal scene of the wounded men dying in mud shown in the cinema might have disturbed his mind, she soon felt that he had "already lost in the mist of death" and she obeyed him as he asked her to leave. She also told the doctor that "she had helped him to endure the suffering as lovingly as she had helped him to discover happiness" (15). She could not report that he was going to commit suicide, as she loved him too much. Dr. Urbino had never heard anything like that and it was a revelation for him when the lady described the history of their love. A long time ago, on a deserted beach in Haiti where the two of them lay naked after love, Jeremiah de Saint-Amour had sighed: "I will never be old." She interpreted it as a heroic determination to struggle against the ravages of time, but he was more specific: he had made the irrevocable decision to take his own life when he was sixty years old. He had turned sixty that year and he set the date as the night before Pentecost, the most important holiday, for taking leave of this world. Once the date was fixed, both of them suffered together the irreparable rush of days that neither of them could stop now. "Jeremiah de Saint-Amour loved life with a senseless passion, he loved the sea and love, he loved his dog and her, and as the date approached he had gradually succumbed to despair as if his death had been not his own decision but an inexorable destiny" (15). This incidence of unnatural death based on some hazy ideas of living gracefully—it is as if old age is disgrace to human beings—is a unique example of love in solitude and solitude in love.

The second incident of death at the beginning of the novel is that of Dr. Juvenal Urbino, who after attending the dead body of Jeremiah de Saint-Amor and having visited the lady in her quarter, came back home and after sometimes when he heard the voice of his lost parrot he climbed up the mango tree to catch it and fell down. His wife Fermina Daza heard the horrified shriek of the servant who saw him falling down and came running to the spot. "He recognized her despite the uproar, through his tears of unrepeatable sorrow at dying without her, and he looked at her for the last and final time with eyes more luminous, more grief-stricken, more grateful than she had ever seen them in half a century of a shared life, and he managed to say to her with his last breath: 'Only God knows how much I loved you'" (42-43). This declaration of love is full of irony as the brief description of their married life has already revealed his solitude in some way. The doctor would regularly get up at the crack of dawn to take his 'secret medicines': potassium bromide to raise his spirits, salicylates for the ache in his bones when it rained, ergosterol drops for vertigo, balladona for sound sleep. He took something every hour always in "secret," because in his long life as doctor and teacher he had always opposed prescribing palliatives for old age. In his pocket he carried a little pad of camphor that he inhaled deeply when no one was watching to calm his fear of so many medicines mixed together. The author's ironic comment that it was easier for him to bear other people's pains than his own throws light on the doctor's selfish nature. But his keeping it a secret from his wife only suggests that their relationship was not based on mutual understanding which is a must for true love. His daily life as described in the novel focuses on his solitude: in the morning he would spend an hour in his study preparing for his class in general medicine; then he bathed, arranged his beard and his hair and took time to look elegant even in eighty one. While taking breakfast he also followed his personal regimen. After coming back from work he ate lunch and had a ten minute siesta, hearing in his sleep the songs of the servant girls and the cries of vendors on the street. Then he read his new books for an hour and then gave lessons to his pet parrot. At four he went out to visit his patients and then it was the time for playing chess or going to cinema with Jeremiah de Saint-Amour. This is the daily routine of a man who is supposed to have little intimate relationship with his wife. Again, though he claimed to be Jeremiah's friend and would meet him regularly, they had never shared their personal joy and grief which friends are supposed to do. The life style of Fermina Daza, the wife of the doctor, too, hardly reveals any hankering for a true conjugal love based on mutual understanding. The author gives a list of a variety of animals which Fermina Daza kept at home, spending the entire day supervising them. Only when a dog was attacked by rabies and started biting other animals, the doctor made a strict rule that the animals that cannot talk would not be allowed to stay in his home. At that time the parrot was purchased and its capacity to talk like a human enchanted the doctor so much that he took the responsibility of training it. Any way, it becomes evident that though the doctor and his wife had observed the golden jubilee celebration of their wedding and besides some quarrels common among the married couples they apparently had a successful life, each of them suffered from 'solitude' in their respective ways.

While the beginning of the novel offers a glimpse into the lives of two couples, one married and the other without any recognized relationship, exposing the inherent solitude in their lives, the rest of the novel depicts, among other things, different phases in the relationship of Florentino Ariza and Fermina Daza, the wife of Dr. Juvenal Urbino. It concentrates first on the juvenile love of Florentino Ariza and Fermina Daza—the affair that survived the aggression of Fermina's father for a long time and when after much suffering Fermina achieves the power to decide, she rebuffed Florentino for being hopeless romantic and married Dr. Juvenal Urbino instead—and the last part is an amazing celebration of love in old age when after a long waiting of fifty-one years, nine months and four days, Florentino Ariza, still a bachelor, utilizes the opportunity of Fermina's widowhood and proclaims his everlasting love for her. Fermina, having social position and established son and daughter, was outraged at the audacity of Florentino but was soon swept away by the flow of Florentino's unconditional love. Different phases in their lives—both at the time of their separation from each other and at the time when they were united, mentally or physically—are rendered from the observation of an omniscient narrator who is objective and amoral. According to Marquez's revelation, the first phase of the love between Florentino Ariza and Fermina Daza was based on the love of his parents Gabriel Eligeo Garcia and Luisa Santiaga Marquez Igoaran. Marquez's maternal grandfather opposed the marriage as unlike his family, Garcia was a recent resident of the town and a supporter of the Conservative. He was also known as a philanderer, the father of four illegitimate children. Garcia wooed Luisa Santiaga with violin serenades, love poems and innumerable letters as Florentino does in the novel. Finally, however, the Colonel accepted Garcia as his son-in-law. The romantic love of Florentino and Fermina who was then a school girl, is based on this real life story. As Marquez explained it in an interview, "The only difference is (my parents) married. And as soon as they were married, they were no longer interesting as literary figures."[4] The love of Florentino Ariza and Fermina Daza in their old age is based on a newspaper story about the death of two Americans of about eighty years of age who were staying with their respective families and yet would meet every year in Acapulco, keeping their extra marital relationship in secret. During one such secret meeting the couple was out in a boat and the boatman murdered the two aged persons with his oars. And because of the murder the romance of two aged persons came to the lime light, evoking discourses on the possibility of love in old age. Marquez was so fascinated by the report that he used the event in his novel as the last part of Florentino- Fermina episode. The novel is not however a love story based on this episode. Rather it is an objective study of love, the most powerful and strongest of all human emotions, in all its possible forms: unrequited love that is love for love's sake; conjugal love which is the outcome of long-term adjustment; jealous love when the lover or the husband cannot tolerate the presence of third person; adulterous love when the married person breaks the marriage vows and loves another person; romantic love at an early age, love in old age, and such others.

Florentino Ariza is rendered as a typical romantic lover who "began his secret life as a solitary hunter" sitting in the most hidden bench in the little park by the side of the road leading to the girls' school only to see Fermina Daza, a school girl holding her bag of books against her chest, pass back and forth four times a day. As she was always accompanied by her elderly spinster aunt, he was denied the slightest opportunity to approach and had to be satisfied with seeing the girl. Little by little he idealized her, endowing her with impossible virtues and imaginary sentiments. He began to write page after page addressing him, but frustrated for not finding a way of sending a letter to her, unburdened himself to his mother. She advised him not to send the letter in the beginning and also told him to win over the girl's aunt. He was then working in Postal Agency and managed to get an opportunity to deliver a telegram to Fermina's father. He tried his best to make him prominent to draw the girl's attention and he was successful in rousing a sense of pity in the girl's mind and also in the mind of her aunt. He was able to hand over his letter to her and was so much immersed in her thought that he was accused of serious charges of neglecting his duty in his work in the Postal Agency. Thanks to an elderly friend his job was saved and he was given the opportunity to play violin in the Cathedral choir. That time his only job was to wait for the reply of the letters. To quote from the novel, "Even when he observed her, unseen, during those days of longing when he waited for a reply to his first letter, he saw her transfigured in the afternoon shimmer of two o'clock in a shower of blossoms from the almond trees where it was always April regardless of the season of the year" (64). The fact was Fermina was still a child who needed time to be passionate. She knew very little about this taciturn suitor "who had appeared in her life like a winter swallow" and whose name she would not even have known if it had not been for his signature on the letter. She was particularly worried because of his determination expressed in his letter. When he demanded her answer with an authority, "that was so different from his languor," she managed to overcome her fear and tried to dodge the issue with her confession that she did not know how to answer him. But Florentino Ariza was not to be shooed away with such excuses. He put so much emotional pressure on her that she had to reply, making him delirious with joy. Then started the phase of mutual understanding, of reciprocated feelings when neither of them could do anything without thinking about the other. They dreamt about each other and waited for letter with the same impatience they felt when they answered them. But While Florentino wrote page after page, imitating his favorite poets from the public library, sometimes going to office without having slept at night, Fermina, under the watchful eye of her father and the vicious spying of the nuns, could barely manage to fill half a page from her notebook. It was also her nature that caused her letters to avoid emotional pitfalls and confine themselves to relating the events of her daily life. "In reality they were distracted letters, intended to keep the coals alive without putting her hand in the fire, while Florentino Ariza burned himself alive in every line. Desperate to infect her with his own madness, he sent her miniaturist's verses inscribed with the point of a pin on camellia petals" (69). Thus from the beginning the basic differences between the two are highlighted so that Fermina's refusal to accept Florentino after three years on the ground that he was a mere romantic fool appears probable.

Florentino Ariza's playing the serenade in his violin intended for Fermina was another example of his imprudence. One day during 'a new civil war,' he was loitering in the road at night playing violin, totally unaware of the imposition of martial law and a six o'clock curfew in the provinces along the Caribbean coast, and was arrested, having been accused of spying. For three nights he had to sleep with irons around his ankles in the cells of the local prison and when he was released he was full of pride for his captivity. Even in his old age he declared himself to be the only man in the country who had "dragged five-pound leg irons for the sake of love." After two years of correspondence, Florentino made direct proposal of marriage to Fermina in a letter of only one paragraph. Fermina had responded to his letters no doubt, but she took everything for lovers' game, without the seriousness of an engagement. Hence she asked for some time to think over the matter. After four months Florentino gave the ultimatum: 'now or never' and Fermina, to get an escape from his accusations, wrote one line reply "I'll marry you if you promise not to make me eat egg plant" which is clearly childish. Though she asked him to keep everything in secret, the matter soon came to her father's notice and the first thing he did was to banish his sister, Fermina's aunt, who had raised her up. He threatened Florentino who was the last man to be afraid and lastly he made a plan to take Fermina to a far away land where she would be forced to forget everything about Florentino. Fermina's father had some miscalculation: the physical distance increased her attraction for Florentino as he was in regular contact with her through telegraphic messages and letters. But it was her experience of suffering on the way and also in that interior land that removed altogether the romantic thoughts that had been injected in her young mind. Before undertaking the journey to an unknown land she managed to write a brief farewell letter to Florentino and for the first time cut off her entire braid at the nape of her neck and rolled it inside the letter. The trip was something she could never have imagined. The first stage along the ridges of the Sierra Nevada, riding mule back in a caravan of Andean mule drivers, lasted eleven days, during which time they were stupefied by the naked sun or drenched by October rains. With no previous experience of riding mule or of staying in inns at night where unknown travelers continuously come and go in darkness, Fermina was almost in a dying condition, suffering from saddle burn and fatigue. After their prolonged stay in Valledupar they continued their journey through the foothills of the mountains and in all the villages they were received by distant relatives. Gradually she learned about herself, felt free for the first time amidst a number of cousins and all this restored her tranquility and her will to live. She also gathered experiences of real life as when she learnt from a relative the idea of arranging the marriage of his daughter to the only heir to the fabulous fortune of Cleofas Moscote. She remembered that she had seen the man in the plazas, "pirouetting his perfect horses with trappings so rich they seemed ornaments used for the Mass, and he was elegant and clever and had a dreamer's eyelashes that could make the stones sigh" (87). And for the first time she compared Florentino Ariza sitting under the little park, with the book of verses in her lap, with another young man. But her mind was still filled up with the ideas of love for

Florentino and with her idealistic attitude and her commitment to binding. So she wanted the consent of her fiancé through telegraphic messages for attending her first adult dance in the town, after her father had granted her the permission.

The basic difference between Florentino and Fermina is further highlighted when Florentino, excited at the idea of an underwater exploration, believed that the treasure of the galleon San Jose were available only twenty meters beneath the surface of the sea and could easily be obtained, Fermina vehemently opposed the idea as she was familiar with the history of the galleon. Her knowledge of real life was far better than that of Florentino who even went as far as requesting his mother to help him financially for exploring the treasure. Fermina knew that the galleon lay beyond the reach of any human being, at a depth of two hundred meters, not the twenty claimed by Florentino. She was also aware of the opinion of some of the members of the Academy of History that the legend of the ship-wrecked galleon had been invented by some brigand of a viceroy to hide his theft of the treasures of the Crown. Yet she celebrated his adventure as a successful one only to satisfy him. But when she continued to receive other letters with still more fantastic details of his adventure, written with as much seriousness as his promises of love, she had to confess to her cousin her fear that her bedazzled sweetheart must have lost his mind. Her return journey after three years was not smooth, though this time her father chose the sea route. She herself was not aware of how much she had matured during the trip until she walked into her closed house and at once undertook the heroic task of making the house livable with the help of one black servant, She was no longer the only child, both spoiled and tyrannized by her father, but "the lady and mistress of an empire of dust and cobwebs that could be saved only by the strength of invincible love" (97). Her exalted courage and strength also moved her father and he delegated to her the authority to run the house on the very night of their return. So when she met Florentino for the first time after her return, she was no more the inexperienced school girl that she had been three years ago but Florentino was still the typical romantic lover he had always been. As they had no opportunity to see each other face to face for a long period of time, they appeared unknown to each other and because of her acquaintance with hard reality and the new responsibility bestowed on her, Fermina could not tolerate the appearance of Florentino whose picture might have been a changed one in her imagination. "She turned her head and saw, a hand's breath from her eyes, those other glacial eyes, that livid face, those lips petrified with fear, just as she had seen them in the crowd at Midnight Mass the first time she was so close to her, but now instead of the commotion of love, she felt the abyss of disenchantment. In an instant the magnitude of her own mistake was revealed to her, and she asked herself, appalled, how she could have nurtured such a chimera in her heart for so long and with so much ferocity" (192). She erased him from her life in no time and showed no weakness even when Florentino's mother managed to have a brief talk with her at her door step. The phase of romantic rapture between the two young persons as rendered in the novel is a clinical analysis of how the cobweb of romanticism may be removed through practical experience of real life as in the case of Fermina. Florentino also changes when as a man he learns how to satisfy his own physical need. Thanks to Marquez's use of exaggerated details in his fiction, Florentino's numerous affairs during the time of fifty years appear absurd, but his vow of having no sexual affair before marrying Fermina is proved false when the revelation came to him that "his illusory love for Fermina Daza could be replaced by an earthly passion" (143). Florentino had affairs with many women none of whom was allowed to occupy the space in his mind that was reserved for Fermina. His affairs were meant for removing his solitude. Besides having affairs with different types of women Florentino also embraced a new way towards solidarity through writing love letters for other men and women who were unable to express themselves in written words. Once he had to write love letters both for the man and the woman who married each other. Out of gratitude they became so close to Florentino that they requested him to be the godfather of their son. After the initial passion of love was diminished, Florentino tried his best to be successful man in profession so that he could be worthy of Fermina, Thus his unrequited love helped him to come out of his solitude through solidarity with common folk and zeal for work.

The married life of Fermina Daza is rendered as an analysis of calculated love—of the patriarchal process of fixing a girl to the yoke of an unknown family and of maintaining a life of social pretention when mutual attraction between the two is almost over after the days of honeymoon. When Fermina's marriage was settled, there was no wastage of time, no waiting for letter. With his degrees of advanced studies in medicine and surgery, his personal charm and family reputation, Juvenal Urbino had been the most desirable of bachelors in the town. He was unaware when he succumbed to the plebeian charm of Fermina Daza. He liked to say that this love was the result of a clinical error. He used to say that he experienced no emotion when he met the woman with whom he would live until the day of his death. "He remembered the sky-blue chemise edged in lace, the feverish eyes, the long hair hanging loose over her shoulders, but he was so concerned with the outbreak of cholera in the colonial district that he took no notice of her flowering adolescence: he had eyes only for the slightest hint that she might be a victim of the plague" (117). Fermina also said in a more explicit way that the young doctor of whom she had heard so much in connection with the cholera epidemic was capable of loving only himself. Dr. Urbino must have felt an attraction towards Fermina and that is whyhe called on her the second day, uninvited, to examine if she was all right. He appeared at the window of her sewing room and signaled her to come over to him and examined her with the required instruments standing there. He also told her that she was like a rose. As her two friends who had been sitting there were laughing at the scene, she got angry and slammed the widow shut. Fermina's father who had noted everything from upper floor, asked the doctor to stop and he compelled Fermina to beg apology to the doctor for slumming the window. She was very angry for being humiliated and hence did not respond to the doctor's letters in which he wanted to know if he would ask his father's permission to talk to her. The letters were brief and she was impressed by their seriousness and simplicity but she could not decide in regard to the reply as she also received some letters of threatening from unknown persons who asked her to get out of the way of Dr. Juvenal Urbino. She felt herself the victim of a great injustice and she also thought that it was all the result of a simple indiscretion on the part of Juvenal Urbino. Her fear increased after receiving a black doll without letter. And her anger revived when her old teacher in the school, the nun who had made her life miserable for an innocent love letter, came as the emissary of love asking her to start going to school and complete the courses. She was intelligent enough to understand that she was sent by Dr. Urbino. To make matters worse her father declared that his business was ruined. This was a time of terrible loneliness for Fermina and she felt blessed to have her cousin Hildebranda, with whom she had been acquainted during the trip, as a guest for few months. Hildebranda was shocked to find her cousin's solitude. In fact Fermina had no life of her own; life was imposed on her from outside in the form of innumerable cores in the house. She was the one who made all the decisions in the house. Whenever she had free time she would iron the linens and kept them in cupboards with lavender, fed the birds or joined the painting class. She knew that she was alone in the world. "She lived in a social limbo" (131). Her former schoolmates were in a heaven that was closed to her after the dishonor of her expulsion. She was "not a neighbor to her neighbors," as her family was a recent settler whose past was known to no body. His father's world was one of traders and stevedores, of war refugees in the public shelter of the Parish Café, of solitary men. Her painting classes alleviated her seclusion somewhat, but the girls who would come were no more than borrowed friends whose affection ended with each class. When Hildebranda thought of arranging a Carnival dance in the house to remove its seclusion, her proposal was of no avail simply because there was no one to invite. On Christian eve Fermina and her cousin went to Midnight Mass in the Cathedral. On the way Fermina showed her all the places where Florentino had been waiting for her and where they met. It is for the first time that she could release herself of her suppressed feelings. While returning home an incident took place that changed the course of Fermina's life. They caught sight of Dr. Urbino who offered them a ride to home and Hildebranda accepted the offer ignoring Fermina's reluctance and Fermina had no other way but to follow her. While riding in the carriage Hildebranda's loose behavior and flirting with the doctor made Fermina furious. When they reached home and said goodbye, the doctor shook their hand and he squeezed Fermina's ring finger telling that he was waiting for reply. The excess of Hildebranda's enthusiasm for Dr. Urbino compelled Fermina to write a brief reply to the doctor's long sent letters, keeping it a secret from her cousin. It did not take much time to announce the engagement of Fermina and Dr. Urbino. Thus their relationship is a perfect example of practical love, meant for its social use.

The suffocated condition of a girl like Fermina in her in-law's house, as rendered in the novel, is a brief analysis of a conjugal life in a respected family. Fermina, who had always been in the habit of making free choices in her father's house despite her father's patriarchal rule, was "caught up more quickly than she had believed in the tangle of conventions and prejudices of her new world" though she did not admit it in her innermost thoughts, or in the "silent arguments she had with her husband during the hours they had once devoted to love" (208). Dr. Urbino justified his own weakness with grave arguments. He would not admit that the difficulties with his wife had their origin in the rarefied air of the house, but blamed them on the very nature of matrimony, "an absurd invention that could exist only by the infinite grace of God." The omniscient narrator's remark in this context is revealing: "The only possible bond was something as improbable and fickle as love, if there was any, and in their case there was none when they married, and when they were on the verge of inventing it, fate had nothing more than confront them with reality" (209). The remark is full of certain well thought views on conjugal life: it has to be based on firm reality; the two persons with their different upbringings, their different views of life and their different habits in day-to-day life have in fact no common ground to share with each other; and these differences may be overlooked only if they are blessed with an illusory (in the sense that it cannot be explained with reference to anything in the mundane world) idea of union of souls (which is the usual meaning of love in married life). Such a blessed condition being very rare, the married couples in respected families are destined to suffer from solitude, sometimes seeking extramarital relationship as did Dr. Urbino. Though both of them were aware of their love in ruins, they always posed to be happy in public. The description of their married life rendered from the perspective of Fermina is full of irony: "Fermina Daza knew then that private life, unlike public life, was fickle and unpredictable. . . . In society she came to be the woman most loved, most cared to, and by the same token most feared, but in nothing was she more demanding or less forgiving than in the management of her house. She always felt as if her life had been lent to her by her husband: she was absolute monarch of a vast empire of happiness, which had been built by him and for him alone. She knew that he loved her above all else, more than anyone else in the world, but only for his own sake: she was in his holy service" (221). This ironic observation may be attributed to the author who sincerely exposed the plight of women in different walks of life.

From the very beginning of *Love in the Time of Cholera* the stigma of love making and marriage in old age has been introduced as a matter of discourse. The novel starts with the suicide of Jeremiah de Saint-Amour who was confident that old age was an indecent state when love making was impossible and so one's life had to be ended before it was too late. Marquez's revolt against the social stigma of love in old age is clearly expressed through Florentino Ariza's conversation with the aged woman Prudencia Pitre and the school girl America Vicuna and finally with the courageous rendering of the love making of Florentino and Fermina in the ship. After the death of Dr. Arbino when Florentino's hope of marrying Fermina was raised, he met Prudencia Pitre. He first met her at a time when she was a widow without child and was ready to receive any man who wanted to be with her. They had established a long and serious relationship and lastly he arranged for her to marry a salesman with whom she had children. That time they talked the entire night and when Florentino wanted to know from her what she would do if someone proposed marriage to her at that age, she directly asked him if he was speaking about Widow Urbino. Though filled with sudden terror, he controlled himself and said that he was talking about him. Thereon she laughed and replied, "Go make fun of your bitch of a mother, may she rest in peace" (287-88). Then she urged him to say what he meant to say, because she knew that he would not have awakened her after so many years of not seeing her just to drink port and eat country bread with pickles. He was looking for someone to cry with, she said. Florentino withdrew in defeat and he walked away trying not to show his tears to others, the tears that "he had been swallowing for fifty one years, nine months and four days" (288). Next he told America Vicuna that he was going to marry. She looked into his eyes with a flash of uncertainty but then recovered and said with a smile that he told a lie because "Old men don't marry" (289). Henceforth he did not want to see her, as he came to full consciousness of both their ages. But the thought of marrying Fermina was not casual. Embracing the crazy idea that he could marry her after the death of her husband, he had been waiting for her since her marriage. During this long period of time he had affairs with a good number of women of different ages and of different social classes as he was in insatiable need of love, but his love for them never went beyond the point where it could "interfere with his determination to remain free for Fermina Daza" (287). The space he kept vacant for Fermina was to be filled with her presence only, and her age had nothing to do in this matter. When Fermina also began to share Florentino's feelings and allowed him to meet her regularly at her home, her daughter Ofelia, among others, opposed this meeting vehemently. She told Fermina that "Florentino Ariza, whose reputation as a pervert was known to everyone, was carrying on an equivalent relationship that did more harm to the family's good name than the villainies of Lorenzo Daza or the ingenuous adventures of Juvenal Urbino" (323). Fermina listened to her without saying a word or without even blinking, but when she finished, Fermina ordered her to live that house immediately and not to set feet there again as long as she lived. Neither the mediation of her son nor the intervention of her friends could break her dissolve. At last she allowed herself to confide to her son-in-law, "A century ago, life screwed that poor man and me because we were too young, and now they want to do the same thing because we are too old" (323). She went as far as to proclaim that the advantage she had as a widow was that there was no man left to give her orders. So she took the independent decision of taking a pleasure cruise along the river. When it was revealed at last that Florentino was also taking a trip in the same vessel, Fermina's son Dr. Urbino glanced at his wife in consternation, with the eyes of a drowning man looking for support, for him, too, like her sister believed that there was an age at which love began to be indecent. Thus the social stigma of love and marriage in old age has been challenged.

Marquez associated excess of passion and disease in a peculiar way which suggests that just as disease is to be controlled through medicine, so also is excessive passion. In *One Hundred Years of Solitude,* Jose Arcadio Buendia commented on his son Aureliano's decision to marry Remedois as love is a disease (63). In *Love in the Time of Cholera,* Florentino's love for Fermina exhibiting the most extreme passion is repeatedly related to disease, and specifically to cholera.[5] Florentino lost his voice, his appetite and his sleep after he saw Fermina for the first time. But when he started waiting for the reply of his first letter, "his anguish was complicated by diarrhea and green vomit, he became disoriented and suffered from sudden fainting spells, and his mother was terrified because his condition did not resemble the turmoil of love so much as the devastation of cholera" (61). When he received the first reply of his letter, his joy knew no bounds. Delirious with joy, Florentino Ariza spent the rest of the afternoon eating roses and reading the note letter by letter, over and over again, and the more he read the more roses he ate, and by midnight he had read it so many times and had eaten so many roses that his mother had to hold his head as if he were a calf and force him to swallow a dose of castor oil" (68). During her trip which was a horrifying torture inflicted on her by her father for loving Florentino, Fermina Daza was also affected by fever which was the result both of her saddle burn as well as fatigue and her love for Florentino and all she needed was a solitary place to cry. During his journey on boat when he was going to join a steamer company service, Florentino had the first sexual experience of his life with Rosalba, a co-passenger, and after he saw her get down the steamer and disappear, he felt alone in the world "and the memory of Fermina Daza, lying in ambush in recent days, dealt him a mortal blow" (145). Jealousy, which until then had been drowned in weeping, took possession of his soul. Florentino sought solace in the thought that during the intoxication of her wedding celebration, Fermina Daza must suffer in those moments when the phantom of the sweetheart she had rejected and humiliated would appear in her thoughts and all her happiness would be destroyed. But this solace did not always work. "But in any case, it was a Saturday of passion, which culminated in a new crisis of fever when he thought the moment had come for the newlyweds to flee in secret through a false door to give themselves over to the delights of their first night. Someone saw him shivering with fever and informed the Captain, who, fearing a case of cholera, left the party with the ship's doctor, and the doctor took the precaution of sending Florentino to the quarantine cabin with a dose of bromides. The next day, however . . . his fever had disappeared" (147). His mother Transito Ariza used to say: "The only disease my son ever had was cholera." The omniscient narrator comments, "She had confused cholera with love, of course, long before her memory failed. But in any event she was mistaken because her son had suffered from six blennorrhagias, although the doctor had said they were not six but the same one that reappeared after each lost battle." (218). Transito Ariza was so much distressed by his son's fever of love, that she even apprehended that it was the same fever when he actually suffered from abscesses. He was so much afraid of drill, that he did not visit the dentist despite his constant toothaches, until the pain became unbearable. "His mother was alarmed by a night of inconsolable moaning from the room next to hers, because these moans seemed to be the same as the ones from another time, which had almost disappeared in the mists of her memory, but when she made him open his mouth to see where love was hurting him, she discovered that he had fallen victim to abscesses" (263). When his patient waiting for more than a year after the demise of Dr. Juvenal Urbino was over and he was received cordially by Fermina who invited him to the terrace in the patio, where it was cooler, he refused in a voice that seemed to like a sigh of sorrow. "He suffered less from the deadly gripping of his bowels than from the thought that she might hear then bubbling. But he managed to endure just an instant longer to say no, he had only passed by to ask her when he might visit" (304). The driver of his car, who after so many years in his service was no longer surprised at anything, asked him to be careful as he suspected Cholera. But Florentino knew that it was his usual ailment. Such postmodern descriptions add a peculiar charm to Marquez's stories.

Juxtaposition of feelings of love and apprehension of death is another characteristic of *Love in the Time of Cholera.* It is also a part of the author's design that Florentino learns about Dr. Juvenal Urbino's death when he was with America Vicuna, the youngest of the women with whom he had affairs. Thought of love and thought of death came together: now that Florentino learnt of Fermina's widowhood, he did not feel the thrill of triumph he had imagined so often in his sleeplessness; instead, he was seized by a terror, "the fantastic realization that it could just as well have been himself for whom the death knell was tolling" (276). Soon, however, Florentino got back his usual stamina, aware that he must utilize the situation for which he had waited as no one else could have done for anything or anyone in this world, "The proof that death had at last interceded on his behalf filled him with the courage he needed to repeat his vow of eternal fidelity and everlasting love to Fermina Daza on her first night of widowhood" (277). After Fermina's strong reaction to his vow of love he understood that it had been a thoughtless and inappropriate act, and for the next two weeks he "suffered a crisis of constipation that swelled his belly like a drum" (277).

He got opportunity to send her letters, unlike any he had ever written, which were "an extensive meditation on life based on his ideas about, and experience of, relations between men and women, which at one time he had intended to write as a complement to the *Lovers' Companion*" (293). Fermina also acknowledged later that those letters were "a meditation on life, love and old age" (299) and Florentino said that those pages "form a book that he would like to write" (308). Gradually he became a regular visitor and his "insatiable need for love overflowed with the illusion of feeling that he was part of a family" (311). One day when Fermina wished to go out for a trip, Florentino offered the idea of a boat journey under the personal care of the captain of the boat. Fermina's son and daughter-in-law went to bid her a good bye and found Florentino there, who, much to their surprise accompanied Fermina, though in a separate cabin. Details of love making of the two aged persons are rendered with seriousness and also fun. At last, they came to realize the meaning of life: "It was as if they had leapt over the arduous Calvary of conjugal life and gone straight to the heart of love. They were together in silence like an old married couple wary of life, beyond the pitfalls of passion, beyond the brutal mockery of hope and the phantoms of disillusion: beyond love, For they had lived together long enough to know that love was always love, any time and any place, but it was more solid the closer it came to death" (345). This realization was possible only because they were travelling in luxurious cabins of a ship, far from the ignoble strife of the madding crowd devoted to money making, sensual satisfaction and social status, far from their relatives and acquaintances ready to console the widow, but kin on spreading scandalous report of the widow's pleasure trip. It was indeed a unique plan devised by the captain of the ship and Florentino Ariza, both having different causes though, to make a trip without stopping, without cargo or passengers, without coming into any port. It was found that the only thing that would allow them to bypass all that was a case of cholera on board. It was decided that the ship would be quarantined and it would hoist the yellow flag and sail in a state of emergency. Everyone knew that the time of cholera had not ended despite all the joyful statistics of the health department and so there was no scope of raising doubts. The passengers were told that there had been a failure, and they were sent on their way on another ship belonging to other company and the cargo was also transferred. Florentino and Fermina were allowed to make love without any fear of being recognized by others. It was a mad voyage "free of trunks, free of social commitments: voyage of love" (345). Thanks to the yellow flag, the ship was asked to leave the bay and go back to the marshes for fear of contamination from cholera patients in the boat. Fermina shuddered as she heard Florentino's voice, "illuminated by the grace of the Holy Spirit": "Let us keep going, going, back to La Dorada." The Captain was stupefied by Florentino's tremendous powers of inspiration. He asked if Forentino meant what he said and the reply was: "I never said anything I did not mean." The Captain now looked at Fermina Daza and saw on her eyelashes the first glimmer of wintry frost. Then he looked at Florentino Ariza, his invincible power, his intrepid love, and "he was overwhelmed by the belated suspicion that it is life, more than death, that has no limits" (348). He further asked Florentino how long they could keep up that coming and going and his answer was "forever." This superb ending at once reveals the mysteries of love, life and death in a nutshell which is simply incomparable.[6]

Of Love and Other Demons (Spanish *Del Amor Y Otros demonios*) , centered on the life of a twelve-year-old girl Sierva Maria, who was bitten by a rabies dog and was taken to a convent instead of a hospital for exorcising, as her case was thought to be one of being possessed by demons. She was kept in a cell and a young priest was given the charge of her treatment. But others protested against the process of treatment and the priest was transferred to a leper hospital. But he could not tolerate that tortures were inflicted on Maria in the name of her treatment. He started coming to the girl secretly at night to recite poems and at last confessed that every moment he was filled with thoughts of her, that everything he ate and drank tasted of her, that she was his life always and everywhere. He also said that the supreme joy of his life was to die with her. Sierva Maria listened to him, "her eyes like those of a startled deer, fixed on him." She only managed to ask, "And now?" and priest Cayetano Dalaura answered, "It is enough for me that you know." He could not go on. Weeping in silence, he slipped his hand beneath her head to serve as a pillow and she curled up at his side. And so they remained, not sleeping, not talking until the rooster began to crow and he had to hurry to arrive in time for 5 o'clock Mass. The meetings at night continued. Sometimes Maria took the initiative, reciting one line of a poem that she had heard so many times and asked him to complete the poem. One day they got exhausted after long recitations and fell asleep. At 5 o'clock the warden brought breakfast and they awoke in alarm only to learn that "life stopped for them." When asked if he was not afraid of being damned, the young priest had the courage to utter that he was already damned but not in the eyes of the Holy Spirit. "I have always believed He attributed more importance to love than to faith," he said. This unique love story of a priest and a twelve-year-old girl centers on the metaphor of love as madness or demonic possession and if one is aware of the logic behind this madness, it would not appear as madness.

Marquez's last fictional writing *Memoirs of My Melancholy Whores* (Spanish *Memorias de mis putas tristes* 2004) contains the most elaborate study on the love of an old man and a virgin of fourteen years. Though this work had to face severe criticism—some even argued that the novella deserves the bad sex award of Britain's *Literary Review*—one cannot miss the typical Marquez style of narration, an ambience of fairytale woven in ideas about time, love, sex and death. The narrator, a columnist for a small-town newspaper, who describes himself as "an ugly, shy, anachronism," is overcome with a desire to sleep with an adolescent virgin on the eve of his ninetieth birthday. To a common human being the desire appears absurd, but to him it was quite natural as his entire life since he achieved manhood was spent for the search for a virgin concubine, the kind of which he had never availed, in the town's brothels where he came in contact with various concubines. They were so many in numbers that he had to maintain a log book which recorded five hundred and fourteen names when he was fifty. He had slept at least once with each of them. To satisfy his latest desire he had already contacted a brothel and the time of his arrival was fixed. But when he came to the brothel and was led to a room, the virgin girl was asleep, drugged with a mixture of bromide and valerian, and looking "as naked and helpless as the she was born." According to Rosa, the brothel keeper, the girl was "beautiful, clean and well mannered, but dying of fear because a friend of hers who had run away with a Stevedore from Gayra bled to death in two hours." Without disturbing her, the old man sat near the girl watching her sleeping body the entire night and at the break of dawn he left the brothel, letting her continue her sleep. This strange meeting was not over with the experience of one night. The old man continued to watch the girl night after night, "counting minute by minute the minutes of the nights that were still left" to him before dying. He discovered that he was in love with the concubine, a new experience that he never had earlier. The rest of the book records the old man's feelings for the adolescent girl and also his recollection of other women in his life. He gave the girl the name Delgadina, the heroine of a medieval ballad that tells the story of a king's incestuous love for his youngest daughter.

Memoirs of My Melancholy Whores is remarkable not for its description of the concubines and the old man's passion, but for the change in the old man's mind after he came in contact with the girl. His memoir, which he wrote after he was immersed in his new found love, is thus a fine example of self analysis. He recorded his discovery about himself: his obsession for having each thing in its right place, each subject at the right time, each word in the right style was not the "well-deserved reward of an ordered mind," but just the opposite. He confessed of having invented "a complete system of pretence" in order to hide the disorder of his nature. He also discovered that he was disciplined not out of virtue but as a reaction to his negligence, that he appeared generous in order to conceal his meanness that he posed to be prudent only because he was evil minded. He also characterized himself as one who cared little about other people's time. All this is due to his realization that "love is not a condition of the spirit but a sign of the zodiac." This novel thus clarifies most of the riddles found in the earlier novels of Marquez. The old narrator solves the enigma of an old man's passion with his comment, "Age is not how old you are but how old you feel." The idea is further elaborated with the words: "We already are old. . . . What happens is that you don't feel it on the inside, but from the outside everybody can see it." The acute suffering of solitude is expressed in the line: "There is no greater misfortune than dying alone." The relation between love and sex is made clear in the observation: "Sex is the consolation you have when you can't have love." Finally, the old man's emphasis on unrequited love, not happy love as such, which alone has invincible power, is suggestive of Marquez's view of love as opposed to solitude. Unrequited love, that is love for love's sake, is also accepted by the author as the most ethical of all acts, and a search for such love has a moral standard of its own and this search is also able to remove solitude.

Notes

1. All the subsequent references to the Nobel Prize acceptance speech are taken from the same source.
2. Angela's love arising out of her free choice is existential in nature. She chose to remain true to herself and this is akin to what Sartre called 'good faith.' Sartre, Jean Paul: *Existentialist Ethics,*
3. Pelayo, Ruben: *Gabriel Garcia Marquez: A Critical Companion,* (2001: Westport: Greenwood Press), p.136
4. Bell-Villada, Gene H. ed. *Conversations with Gabriel Garcia Marquez,* (Jackson: University Press of Mississippi, 2006), p.156
5. The term 'cholera' which is used in Spanish as 'colera' can also denote passion and rage. The English objective choleric has the same meaning. Considering this meaning the title is a pun, cholera as the disease and cholera as passion. This observation is attached to the central question of the book: Is love helped or hindered by extreme passion? *Wikipedia.org.Love.in.the.time.of.cholera.*
6. Thanks to the unique technique of story-telling, both the juvenile love and the love in old age are realistically portrayed. The distinguishing marks of Marquez's delineation of this amazing story are (1) his sense of humor even when describing a serious matter, (2) a rare combination of socio-political condition of Colombia—the time of Civil War, spread of epidemic such as cholera and the patriarchal rule in family—and personal love,(3)his embracing postmodern technique that at once differentiates the love in the novel from traditional romantic love, (4) use of fantasy in a limited way and above all, (5) the magic of his language. The novel is in fact a clinical analysis of different types of love: love of jealousy as when Olimpia Zuleta, a pigeon fancier, was killed by her husband who came to know of her sexual relationship with Florentino; love between an old man and an adolescent girl as in the case of the school girl America and Florentino; the uninhibited love of honeymoon, a short term love enjoyed in Paris by Florentino and Fermina; conjugal love of pretension experienced by Dr. Urbino and Fermina; love that stretches beyond centuries as conceived by Florentino, and such others. The narrator describes all this in a funny way; and when he takes up some serious affair it

usually co-exists with revelation of some stark reality. The passion of juvenile love is described metaphorically to point out the basic differences between the girl and the young man: Fermina, "under the watchful eye of her father and the vicious spying of the nuns, could barely manage to fill half a page" and her letters were in reality "distracted letters, intended to keep the coals alive without her hand in the fire, while Florentino Ariza burned himself alive in every line" (69). Marquez describes in detail the terrifying Civil War that intrudes into the love affair. Juxtaposition of the grim reality of civil war and personal love affair adds charm to Marquez's fiction which concentrates on solitude to which human being is condemned, and on solidarity and love to which the solitary person aspires, often knowing that these are unattainable in real life.

Garcia Marquez's Social Concerns and his Journalistic Zeal

Gabriel Garcia Marquez was one of the few successful writers of the world who continued to work as a columnist even after reaching the glorious height a writer of fiction ever dreams of attaining. Once asked in a *Paris Review Interview* in 1983 about the differences between fiction and journalistic writing, Marquez said, "Nothing. I don't think there is any difference. The sources are the same, the material is the same, and the resources are the same" (*www.theparis review. org./interviews/3196/theartoffiction-69-gabriel-garcia-marquez).* He further said that in journalism just one fact that is false prejudices the entire work and in fiction one single fact that is true gives legitimacy to the entire work, and what is required of the writer is his commitment. Marquez was committed to truth while writing his fiction, be it expressed in dense mythology and wrapped in fantasy or in the dry rationalist discourse. Though in most of his fictional writings the focus is on the political situation of Latin America, the social condition of the continent, and particularly of his homeland Colombia, looms large. This is a society devastated by economic exploitations, civil wars and autocratic rules. Without any authorial comment the evils of the society are exposed through ironic and exaggerated rendering. To quote George McMurray's comment on Marquez in this context, "For him the duty of the revolutionary writer is to write well and the ideal novel is one that moves its readers by its social and political content, and at the same time, by its power to penetrate reality and expose its other side."[1]

Garcia Marquez's fictional writings are not imitation of real life the kind of which is found in the realistic novels based on the western model, but they offer a thorough analysis of the social systems and of the values on which the social norms are based in the Latin American countries in general and in Colombia in particular. It is a society of multiple races including the natives as well as the outsiders some of whom had come centuries ago and some being recent immigrants. But there is no racial conflict; people are mostly Catholics and nobody bothered about the linguistic differences. Though Marquez's chief concern is political—he concentrated on the dictatorial rules in different countries of Latin America both in his fiction and in journalistic writing—his concern for the society arrests the readers' attention. The society portrayed in his writing is one that has been devastated by fighting among political opponents at the cost of the lives of the innocents, oppression inflicted on the mass by dictatorial regimes, economic exploitations made by multinational companied, practice of giving and taking bribes, superstitions and meaningless customs. *In Evil Hour* starts with a social problem—the problem of putting up lampoons by unknown persons for tarnishing some well-off persons in the society. Whatever be the ultimate purpose of those lampoons, the first victim of the process of tarnishing was an innocent musician. It was written in a piece of paper stuck to the door of a rich man Cesar Montero that his wife was having an affair with the musician Pastor who composed songs dedicated to her. Cesar Montero was going out in the morning, telling his wife that he would come back on Saturday and after he climbed up his mule, he saw the paper stuck to the door of his house. He did not think it necessary to discuss the matter with his wife—he had already heard the song that was sung all night long and had also seen his wife following the melody in a low voice—but went straight to Pastor's home. Pastor was taken aback and stood still, his mouth open, when he saw Cesar Montero with his heels planted on the earthen floor and the shotgun at waist level pointed at him. Montero clenched the trigger without a word and Pastor was seen "dragging himself with the undulation of a worm along a furrow of tiny bloody feathers" (8). This picture of bloodshed in the very first chapter of the book holds up the picture of a society that was actually passing through evil hours. It is soon learnt that Pastor had composed the music not for Montero's wife, but for his own beloved whom he was to marry soon. His love was kept a secret and he had to sacrifice his life for this secrecy; it was as if the society had the authority to be well informed beforehand of the identity of the person to whom an artist's song was dedicated. Cesar Montero being a rich man, the mayor took the opportunity to exploit him in the name of collecting funds for his party. It was a society in which a murderer would be pardoned if it were a case of honor killing and if for extra protection enough money were spent as bribe by the murderer. After Pepe Amador, the innocent boy, had been killed in police custody and the mayor was trying to push up the case, Pepe's mother accompanied by other women came to the police barrack in search of Pepe and the mayor drove them away in the most inhuman way, "A woman with her arms open came along in the middle of the street, running in the opposite direction. There were flying ants in the clean air. Still not knowing what was going on, the mayor upholstered his revolver and started to run. A group of women was trying to force the door of the barracks. Several men were struggling with them to keep them out. The mayor beat them away, put his back against the door, and aimed at all of them. "I'll drop anyone who takes a step." A policeman who'd been holding it from inside then opened the door, with his rifle at the ready, and blew his whistle. Two other policemen ran out onto the balcony, fired several shots in the air, and the group scattered to the ends of the street. At that moment, howling like a dog, the woman appeared on the corner. The mayor recognized Pepe Amador's mother. He gave a leap inside the barracks and from the stairway ordered the policeman: "Take charge of that woman" (175). The torture inflicted on the poor mother, murders in police barracks and the government's denial of the truth, bribes taken openly for relieving the murderer of the charge leveled against him; killing of innocents and such others are faithfully recorded in the book, providing the readers with the details of the bad time that overpowered the society. It was the time of social disorder in Colombia preceding *la violencia.*

Though *One Hundred Years of Solitude* concentrates on constructing national history in its own way of fusing fantasy and realism, starting from the end of colonial rule to the days of the exploitation of the North American Fruit Company, it also focuses on what commonly goes by the name of social realism. After the armistice of Neerlanda the local authorities were mayors without initiatives, decorative judges picked up from among the peaceful and retired conservatives. With the arrival of the North American Fruit Company some of the local functionaries were replaced by officers of the Fruit Company who had less sympathy for the local people. "The old policemen were replaced by hired assassins with machetes" (196). These new policemen brought a reign of terror. Common people were killed for no valid reason. A seven-year-old child was brutally killed for having accidentally bumped into a corporal of police and for having spilled a bottle of soft drink on the police man's uniform, The boy's grandfather was also beheaded when he tried to stop the policeman (196). The narrator only presents the facts in an objective way displaying little emotion, and when he makes any comment, it is loaded with irony. "The only difference to-day between liberals and conservatives is that the liberals go to mass at five o'clock and the conservatives at eight" (299). What the narrator does not say and what is implied in the comment is that the common mass suffered in the same way under both the regimes. The novel clearly depicts how the non-functioning of government offices brought misery in the lives of the common people: "After the armistice of Neerlanda while colonel Aureliano Buendia took refuge with his little gold fishes, he kept in touch with the rebel officers who had been faithful to him until the defeat. With them he waged the sad war of daily humiliation, of entreaties and petitions, of come-back-tomorrow, of any-time-now, of we-are-studying-your-case with the proper attention, the war hopelessly lost against the many yours-most-trulys who should have signed and would never sign the life-time pensions. The other war, the bloody one of twenty years did not cause them as much damage as the corrosive war of eternal postponements"(200). Even Colonel Gerineldo Marquez, who escaped three attempts on his life, survived five wounds, and emerged unscathed from innumerable battles, succumbed to that atrocious siege of waiting and sank into miserable defeat of old age.

One Hundred Years of Solitude also reveals how the Latin American society developed bourgeois class consciousness which was the obvious result of the decline of the rural way of life. Earlier there had hardly been any hierarchy of social status but the scenario was changed after the arrival of the North American fruit company in Colombia. A self conscious society lady could no more accept the wedding of her daughter with a mechanic. When Aureliano Segundo's wife Fernanda del Carpio suspected that her daughter Meme was involved in love affair, she immediately investigated the matter herself and caught her daughter red handed inside the cinema hall. She managed to hear the man's tremulous voice in the midst of the deafening shouts and laughter of the audience; 'I am sorry, love,' she heard him say. She took Meme out of the place without saying a word to her, put her through the shame of parading along the noisy Street of the Turks, and locked her in her bedroom. On the following day at the six in afternoon, when the man called on her, Fernanda recognized the voice and had a full view of the young man, sallow with dark and melancholy eyes. "He was wearing a shabby linen suit with shoes that showed the desperate defense of superimposed patches of white zinc, and in his hand he was carrying a straw that he had bought the Saturday before. In all his life he could never have been as frightened as at that moment, but he had a dignity and presence that spared him from humiliation and a genuine elegance that was defeated only by tarnished hands and nails that had been shattered by rough work"(232). Fernanda, however, needed only one look to guess "his status of mechanic." She saw that he was wearing his one Sunday suit and that underneath his shirt he bore the rash of the banana company. She would not let him speak and would not even let him come through the door, as it was beyond her imagination that a society lady like her could have a decent talk with a mechanic. So she used harsh words to drive him away. 'Go away. You've got no reason to come calling on any decent person,' she said. His name was Mauricio Babilonia. Born and brought up in Macondo, he was now an apprentice mechanic in the banana company garage. Meme had met him by chance one afternoon when he was assigned the duty of a chauffeur, as the regular chauffeur was sick that day. After that there were occasions to meet and they fell in love. Her love was so anchored in the depth of her mind that it did not diminish after so much suffering. When her mother ceased to suspect that she was still involved in love, she met Mauricio Babilonia every evening in the bathroom where he entered, lifting up the tiles of the roof. One evening Fernanda suspected that something was going on and took immediate steps. On the next day she invited the new mayor, who like her had come down from the highlands, to lunch and asked him to station a guard in the backyard to stop stealing of hens. That night the guard shot Mauricio as he was found lifting up the tiles. "A bullet lodged in the spinal column reduced him to his bed for the rest of his life" (238). The severe punishment inflicted on him is the proof of how the marginalized in the Colombian society was vulnerable to false accusations and condemnation after the society became commercialized.

In general, the contemporary society as rendered in Marquez's fiction is a permissive society in which there is no taboo in making conjugal relationship between different races. During the eighteenth and the nineteenth centuries the society did not much bother about extra marital relationships and illegitimate children. In *One Hundred Years of Solitude* all the seventeen sons of Colonel Aureliano Buendia born of seventeen different women came to his mother Ursula to be baptized, and Ursula who strongly protested all acts she thought immoral, not sparing even her most influential son Aureliano, saw nothing to grumble in the process of baptizing and in their acquiring the title of Buendia. The novel clearly reveals that the establishment of the churches and the priests' emphasis on marriage to make everything legal eventually created social pretences and the problem of illegitimate children. Marquez's view is clear: it is the European concept of civilization based on law that had been imposed on the Latin American culture and this imposition is the root cause of the socio-cultural problems of the land including social pretence. *In Evil Hour* exposes this social pretence side by side the political condition. At the time of confession Father Angel came to know that the woman who was known as Judge Arcadio's wife was not married at all. Father Angel had been insisting her on their marriage for last six months without any effect and he repeated it again. And again Judge Arcadio's wife said, "No hope at all, Father. Even less now that I'm going to have a child." Alarmed and almost horrified, he said that in that case the baby would be illegitimate. Least concerned with legitimacy, the woman answered, "That doesn't matter. Arcadio treats me well now. If I make him marry me, then he'll feel tied down and make me pay for it" (70). As Father Angel remained silent, she repeated, "No hope at all, Father. Don Sabas bought me for two hundred pesos, sucked my juice out in three months, and then threw me into the street without a pin. If Arcadio had not taken me in, I would have starved to death . . . or I would have had to become a whore" (70-71). That she hardly had any alternative other than remaining with the judge without marital status and living the miserable life of a whore and that too, just for her survival, speaks volume of the poverty in the land. Father Angel made fresh attempts, telling her that the way she was living not only left her in a precarious situation, but created a bad example for the town. He also said that the woman should legitimize her situation and keep her away from the gossiping tongues. Thereon the woman told him that as she always did things in broad daylight, nobody bothered about her activities, and that is why nobody had wasted his time putting any lampoon on her door. The woman thus throws light on the fact that the lampoons pasted on the doors of the influential persons of the time had their roots in the pretences of those persons who maintained a double standard of life, one open and the other secret. As was the lampoon about Raquel Contreres about whom it was written that the trips she had taken were not to get her dentures fitted, but to get an abortion. Judge Arcadio said that the lampoon was not necessary as everybody was aware of the fact. Marquez's point is that whether everybody knew about the scandal is not the matter; the scandal was due to the secrecy, the pretence maintained by the woman concerned. It must be noted that Marquez was least concerned with the moral codes maintained in society. His approach is amoral and humanistic. His concern with social pretences is not therefore related to moral prejudices but to the very essence of human life. As a humanist he expects that everyone must be true to oneself.

What troubled Marquez more than anything else was the system of prostitution in Latin American society that had prevailed since ages. In *One Hundred Years of Solitude,* the author describes from the perspective of adolescent Aureliano Buendia the inhuman torture inflicted on a prostitute girl.

Auriliano went to Catarino's store to listen the old traveler Francisco whose profession was to relate the things that had happened in the places along his route. When Aureliano was coming back, a fat woman on a rocking chair who had accompanied Francisco this time signaled him with her hand and asked him to give her twenty cents and enter an adjacent room. Not knowing why he was called, Aureliano entered the room having thrown twenty cents. And he found a naked adolescent mulatto girl on a bed. "Before Aureliano sixty three men had passed through the room that night. From being used too much, kneaded with sweat and sighs, the air in the room had begun to turn to mud. The girl took off the soaked sheet and asked Aureliano to hold it by one side. It was as heavy as a piece of canvas. They squeezed it, twisting it at the ends until it regained its natural weight. They turned over the mat and the sweat came out of the other side. Aureliano was anxious for that operation never to end. He knew theoretical mechanics of love, but he could not stay on his feet because of the weakness of his knees. . . In spite of the girl's efforts he felt more and more indifferent and terribly alone. 'I'll throw in another twenty cents,' he said with a desolate voice. The girl thanked him in silence. Her back was raw. Her skin was stuck to her ribs and her breathing was forced because of an immeasurable exhaustion" (50) No authorial comment is necessary to point at the plight of the girl and at the old matron's greed that polluted the society drawing innocent boys to the ancient and sadistic game of human race the kind of which is not found in any other animal society. The girl had been forced to be a prostitute two years ago by her grandmother who carried her from town to town, putting her to bed for twenty cents each time in order to make up the value of her burned house that had been put to ashes for her falling asleep without putting out the candle. The same story we find in elaborated form in 'The Incredible and sad story of Innocent Erendira and her Heartless Grandmother.' The details of the grandmother—she was rescued from a house of prostitution in the Antilles by Amadis, the grandfather of Erendira, and was transplanted "forever in the impunity of the desert"—and of Erendira's service to her as a bonded labor as well as the destruction caused by the fire are given in the story. Erendira was first taken to a widower who was well known in the locality for "the price he paid for virginity" and after bargaining he was ready to give one hundred and fifty pesos for the virgin girl. It is indeed difficult to give an objective rendering of how she was handled by the widower and only a great writer like Marquez can do it, stupefying the readers. "At the widower's first attempt, Erendira shouted something inaudible and tried to get away. The widower answered her without any voice, twisted her arm by the wrist, and dragged her to the hammock. She fought him off with a scratch on the face and shouted in silence again, but he replied with a solemn slap which lifted her off the ground and suspended her in the air for an instant with her long Medusa hair floating in space. He grabbed her about the waist before she touched ground again, flung her into the hammock with a brutal heave, and held her down with her knees. Erendira then succumbed to the terror, lost consciousness, and as if fascinated by the moonbeams from a fish that was floating through the storm air. . ." (CS, 250). When there was no man left in the village that could pay anything for Erendira's love, her grandmother put her on a truck and moved from one town to another where customers were available. It is no doubt an exaggerated version of fact—hyperbole was one of the techniques used by Marquez for bringing the desired effect in his fiction—and the presence of one fact, that is the intolerable suffering of bonded sex labor, brings the fiction close to reality. Marquez is able to affect the mind of his readers with such renderings of tortured girls who live in the margin and utter poverty of the people need not even be mentioned.

Portraits of women in a society reveal the condition of that society better than anything else and Marquez's social concern is also best revealed through the portraits of women in his fictional writings. Besides the prostitutes, there are broadly, two other categories of women in Marquez's fiction: a) women belonging to middle class and upper middle class sections of the society who are mostly housewives and b) the working class women. Of all the women characters created by Marquez in his fictional writings Ursula is unique for her outstanding organizing capacity, her physical and mental stamina—she and her husband were the founders of Macondo and after her husband got insane, she took the responsibility not only of the extended Buendia family but of the entire town—and her strong moral sense and her humanistic concern. It is likely that Marquez intended to give the message that before the western civilization and the authority of the church had a strong hold on the Latin American villages and the villagers had their freedom to live according to their own norms, the women also had the privilege to show their strength in different social functions. Thus we find that after Aureliano had left Macondo and became a great leader of the Revolutionaries and Arcadio got the opportunity to terrorize the mayor, assaulting his house and dragging him out, Ursula came running to the spot to control the situation. She whipped Arcadio without mercy and chased him to the back of the courtyard, where Arcadio "curled up like a snail in its shell." The mayor lay unconscious, tied to a post. The boys in the squad were scattered as they feared that Ursula would chase them too. But she did not even look at them. She untied the mayor and took him home. Before leaving the headquarter she released the prisoners from the stocks. From that time on Ursula was the one "who ruled in the town. She reestablished Sunday Mass, suspended the use of red armbands, and abrogated the harebrained decrees" (93). During the time of war when Aureliano hardly came to Macondo, Ursula got the seventeen sons of Aureliano baptized with the name of Aureliano and the last name of the mother. She jotted down in a ledger the name and address of the mother of each child and also the child's date of birth and the name of the place where the child was born. After the surrender of Colonel Aureliano Buendia and after he survived the bullet injury while attempting to commit suicide, Ursula rejuvenated the house again with a vitality that seemed impossible at her age. She had the house washed and painted, changed the furniture, restored the garden and planted new flowers. She also assigned duty to the soldiers who had been appointed by the government for guarding the house. She invited them to eat, gave them clothing, and taught them how to read and write. When the government withdrew the guard, one of them continued living in the house and was in her service for many years. Her dominating presence in the novel and her physical and moral strength are not found in any other woman character in Marquez's fictional world. She was created as an ideal woman character the like of who is hardly seen in the present society as the society at present is unable to nourish such a character.

In some of his fictional writings Marquez's strong disapproval of beauty contests modeled on the western practice of such contests is suggested. When the life of the common people is almost devastated by utter poverty, the autocratic ruler arranges beauty contests and spends a lot of money on these. In *The Autumn of the Patriarch* Marquez satirically calls the beauty queen "the beauty queen of the poor, an incredible creature from that miserable wallow," known as the dog fight district. The dictator would receive the beauty queen in a special audience and would dance the first waltz with her. And everything was to be published in the newspaper so that this kind of crap would make a big hit with the poor. With the use of hyperbole Marquez describes how the old dictator, supposed to be in love with the beauty queen, Manuela Sanchez, would take with him various gifts for her including clocks, sewing machines, music boxes and what not and how her house being filled up with the gifts, they had to take over the houses next door and knock down the intervening walls in order to have rooms for them. The ludicrous description intends to satirize the wastage of money which could be used for eradicating poverty. Bayardo San Roman's mother Alberta Simonds in *Chronicle of a Death Foretold* is introduced as beauty queen of her time, "a big mulatto woman from Curacao, who spoke Spanish with a mixture of Papiamento, in her youth had been proclaimed the most beautiful of the of the two hundred most beautiful women of the Antilles" (32-33). She was the wife of General Petronio San Romain, one of the major glories of the Conservative regime for having put Colonel Aureliano Buendia to flight in the disaster of Tucurinca. In a very innocent way the narrator brackets the Conservative regime and the beauty contest, and the irony lies in the fact that such an 'enlightened' family supported the superstitious custom of returning the bride to her parents on the very night of the marriage for her failure to prove her virginity through a process that is unscientific and absurd. According to the prevailing social custom, the marital status of the women belonging to the middle class and upper middle class families depended on the proof of virginity of the bride on the night of her marriage. As it is quite natural, the girls were not able to prove their virginity in the crude way it was demanded from them. Hence the women invented the way of deceiving their husbands and every girl was trained by her elderly friends in that art of deceiving. Angela Vicario did not like to deceive her husband and so she did not learn the trick. But her husband Bayardo San Roman demanded the proof and when he did not get it, he returned his wife immediately to her parents and she had to undergo utter humiliation and torture. Just after she was returned, Angela's mother Pura Vicario held her by the hair with one hand and started beating her with the other with such a rage that it seemed that she was going to kill her daughter. Angela's two brothers were summoned by her mother. They found Angela lying face down on the dining room coach, her face bruised. Pedro Vicario held her up into the air by the waist and made her sit on the dining room table. Trembling with rage he wanted to know the name of the man who had seduced her. According to the custom, if a bride was returned for her inability to show proof of her virginity, it was a great dishonor to the bride's family and to revive their honor they were to kill the girl's seducer as it was taken for granted that a girl unable to prove her virginity must have been seduced by one. No one was ready to change the barbaric custom and to think scientifically that proof of virginity was just a myth. The novel offers enough scope to think that there was in fact no seducer and that Angela having been terrified that the severe beating inflicted on her would not stop until a seducer's name would be disclosed, she just uttered the name of Santiago Nasar, the name that first came to her mind. Santiago had been well known in the locality for seducing street-side girls but never had attempted any girl belonging to the upper class. So everybody was astonished, but once his name was uttered, there was no other option for the Vicario brothers but to kill him, thanks to the force of the custom. So Pedro and Pablo Vicario were entrusted with the responsibility of keeping the honor of the family by killing Santiago Nasar. And nobody stopped them or even informed Nasar of their decision. The narrator informs that Clotilde Armenta was certain that the Vicario brothers "were not as anxious to fulfill the sentence as to find someone who would do them the favor of stopping them" (57)[2]. Even the mayor took no step when he was informed that the Vicario brothers were getting ready in public for the murder on the plea that he was unable to take any step before anything happened. And after the murder was actually done, the mayor had an emergency conversation with the governor of the province and the latter authorized him to take the preliminary steps while he sent an investigating officer. Marquez does not say that such type of killing was a regular happening there, but one such incident is enough to highlight the moral chaos through which the society was proceeding. He reveals the callousness of the people, blinded by prejudices, and their inability to differentiate between right and wrong. It was a society that allowed its boys to go to the prostitutes, but demanded proof of virginity from the young bride.

The torture inflicted on the women belonging to the middle class is further elaborated in the secluded life of Agela Vicario after she was returned by her husband. The entire Vicario family was compelled to leave the town and Angela had to live alone with her mother who had gone beyond what was possible to make her die in life. The image of the secluded woman captured in lucid language by the narrator may be quoted: "At the window of the house that faced the sea, embroidering by machine during the hottest hour of the day, was a woman half in mourning, with steel-rimmed glasses and yellowish gray hair, and hanging above her head was a cage with a cannery that didn't stop singing. .It was she: Angela Vicario, twenty-three years after the drama" (89). This secluded picture of an innocent woman, prematurely aged, is set against a society that was prejudiced, deceitful and cruel. In this society everyone was expected to be deceitful to keep up the norm. Angela also could very well escape all the hazards if she would follow the advice of her elderly friends and use some tricks to prove her virginity. But a person who has self respect and decency like Angela abhors such deceitfulness and has to pay a heavy price for her free choice. While the dictatorial rule curbs the physical freedom of the persons, social prejudices curb their spiritual freedom. Marquez offers a picture of the society where human beings are rendered as puppets, unaffected by moral laxity and deceitfulness. In *Love in the Time of Cholera,* the description of Sara Noriega, with whom Florentino Ariza had an affair for a period of time, offers a realistic picture of the society: "(She) had enjoyed fifteen minutes of fame in her youth when she won a competition with a collection of poems about love among the poor, a book that was never published. She was a teacher of deportment and civics in the public schools, and she lived on her salary in a rented flat . . . in the old Gethsemane District. She had had several occasional lovers, but none with matrimony, because it was difficult for a man of her time and place to marry a woman he had taken to bed. Nor did she cherish that dream again after her first formal fiancé, whom she loved with the almost demented passion of which one is capable at the age of eighteen, broke the engagement one week before the date they had set for the wedding, and left her to wander the limbo of abandoned brides or of used goods, as they used to say in those days" (197). The paragraph quoted above is a direct comment on the plight of women, even educated women with job, who were denied equal treatment in a male dominated society of Latin America. Marquez displays his deep social concern through such occasional remarks, devoid of passion.

Marquez's assessment of married life, particularly one that is not based on mutual love, is as sharp as that of a feminist. The relation between Ursula and Jose Arcadio Buendia in *One Hundred Years of Solitude* is acknowledged by the author as one based on something greater than what usually goes by the word 'love': "(They) were joined till death by a bond that was more solid than love: a common prick of conscience"(23). The history of the development of different families in Caribbean region through in-breeding and cross-breeding among different races is rendered in the novel and this history throws much light on the social patterns and hierarchies in the area. Ursula's ancestor, an Aragonese merchant in Riohacha, left Riohacha and came to a peaceful Indian settlement located in the foothills. There he started partnership business with a native born tobacco planter who ancestor of Jose Arcadio Buendia. That was a lucrative partnership and both the parties were able to make fortune. Several centuries later when Uesula and Jose Arcadio Buendia decided to marry, their relatives opposed in the beginning, but later gave consent. After their marriage there was a mishap. Jose Arcadio Buendia killed a man in a duel and both of them suffered from biting of conscience. They saw the dead man regularly in their home and vexed, they left their village in search of a new settlement. After a long and tedious journey they established a new settlement and called it Macondo. Both of them, devoted to each other in their own ways, took the responsibility of their family and also of the village and Ursula proved herself more practical than her husband, while Jose Arcadio was swept by the ideas of new inventions and got crazy. Their life pattern, set in earlier days and designed in epic form, had hardly any scope to express conventional love for each other and hence the narrator rightly observes that they were joined by a thread more solid than love. In the fictional world of Marquez married women are often the silent workers who sacrifice them for the family. For example, Angela Vicario's mother in *Chronicle of a Death Foretold*: "Purisma del Carman . . . had been a school teacher until she married forever. Her meek and somewhat afflicted look hid the strength of her character quite well. 'She looked like a nun,' Mercedes recalls. She devoted herself with such spirit of sacrifice to the care of her husband and the rearing of children that at times one forgot she still existed"(30).

Marquez's rendering of married life in affluent families as revealed in *Love in the Time of Cholera* gives a realistic picture of the society and also exposes Marquez's almost feminist concern. Having described how Fermina Daza felt suffocated in her in-law's house after coming back from Europe where they spent their time of honeymoon the narrator gives his own comment along with Dr. Urbino's views on the matter. "It was against all scientific reason for two people who hardly knew each other, with no ties at all between them, with different characters, different upbringings and even different genders, to suddenly find themselves committed to living together, to sleeping in the same bed, to sharing two destinies that perhaps were fated to go in opposite directions. He would say: 'The problem with marriage is that it ends every night after making love, and it must be rebuilt every morning before breakfast.' And worst of all was theirs, arising out of two opposing classes, in a city that still dreamed of the return of the Viceroys. The only possible bond was something as improbable and fickle as love, if there was any, and in their case there was none when they married, and they were on the verge of inventing it, fate had done nothing more than confront them with reality" (209). They developed the art of pretence and played the role of the happiest couple in public. They were different from others in the society and they were modern, and for that reason transgressors against the traditional order. Fermina Daza learnt that life in the world, which had caused her so much uncertainty before she was familiar with it, was nothing more than a system of atavistic contracts, "banal ceremonies, preordained words, with which people entertained each other in society in order not to commit murder." Fermina Daza learnt that the problem in public life is learning to overcome terror and the problem in married life is to overcome boredom. She made this discovery with the clarity of a revelation when she entered the vast salon of the Social Club, "where the air was thin with mingled scent of so many flowers, the brilliance of the waltzes, the tumult of perspiring men and tremendous women who looked at her not knowing how they were going to exorcise the dazzling menace that had come to them from the outside world" (211). Instead of frightening them even more, as she was always doing, she had the compassion to help them learn to know her. She found that they were no different from what she wanted them to be. Dr. Urbino also on his part commanded respect from others, as he used his intelligence and calculated solemnity. During all the social occasions such as civic exhibitions, the Poetic Festival, artistic events, charity raffles, patriotic ceremonies and the first journey in a balloon, Fermina Daza and Dr. Urbino were in the forefront. Though they were continuing a loveless conjugal life, "no one could have imagined any one happier than they or a marriage more harmonious than theirs." During this time Fermina used the house left by her father as a "refuge from the asphyxiation of the family palace." As soon as she could escape from public view, she would go in secret to the Park of the Evangels to visit some old friends or to get new ones.

While women belonging to upper class could somehow remove the loneliness and boredom of their loveless married life, a poor married woman had no such freedom. Thus Olimpia Zuleta was murdered by her husband immediately after he came to know of her affair with Florentino, an affair that had beckoned her with the hope of getting a refuge from her loveless married life. Here was the brute force of the patriarchal society that demanded total surrender, both physical and mental, of a wife. Marquez has also rendered cases of gender-related oppression which are intersected by factors such as class and caste. In *Chronicle of a Death Foretold,* Victoria Guzman, the cook in Santiago Nasar's house, was a victim of sexual oppression at the hands of the upper class of men. She had been seduced by Ibrahim Nasar in the fullness of her adolescence. She had made love to him in secret for several years in the stables of the ranch, and he brought her to be a servant when the affection was over. Divina Flor, who was the daughter of her recent mate, knew that she was destined for Santiago Nasar's furtive bed and that idea brought out a premature anxiety in her. But Victoria Guzman had the courage to threaten Santiago Nasar with a blood-stained knife when Santiago held the wrist of her daughter, Divina Flor. She remembered Santiago Nasar's horror when she pulled out the insides of a rabbit by the roots and threw the steaming guts to the dogs. Though Santiago asked her not to be a savage, she continued feeding the dog; "she had so many postponed rages the morning of the crime" that she liked to embitter Santiago's breakfast. There are suggestions in the book that she did not inform Santiago Nasar of the Vicario brothers' plan to murder him and also kept his mother ignorant of this development. After four o'clock, when (Clotilde Armanta) saw the lights on in the kitchen of Placida Linero's house, she sent the last urgent message to Victoria Guzman by the beggar woman who came by everyday to ask for a little milk in the name of charity"(58). The mishap might be avoided in case Santiago Nasar could be informed of the preparation for murder beforehand. But nobody including the cook Victoria Guzman informed him. Anyway, such incident shows that the suppressed anger of the poor woman against the rich men characterizes the class-torn society of Colombia, as it does anywhere else in the world.

Of Love and Other Demons displays a real picture of Latin American society during eighteenth century. It begins with a note in which the narrator demands that he was present at a convent when it was being emptied because the area of the convent had been selected as the space where a luxury hotel would be built up. Laborers unearthed "three generations of bishops and abbesses and other eminent personages" and at last they found the tomb of a twelve-year-old girl called Sierva Maria de Todos Los Angeles. Her hair of the color of copper flowed out of her head twenty meters long and it was supposed that her hair continued to grow after her death. This note is followed by the story that centers on Maria who survived two hundred years ago. The history of her family learnt from the novella throws much light on the society of the time. Maria's father the Marquis had loved an insane woman but was forced to marry another. Maria, the daughter of liaison, was left to the care of African slaves and she naturally picked up various African languages and African behavior. On her twelfth birthday she was taken to the market by a slave and a dog bit her slightly after biting several persons. Next day the dog died and the servants reported that it was a rabies dog. Maria's father did not pay heed to the words of the slave and the slaves began their treatment on the girl in their own ways. Thanks to irrational superstitions prevalent at that time, Maria was considered possessed by demons and her father left her to the convent of Santa Clara for being exorcised. As was the rule of the church, the poor girl was kept imprisoned in a cell and a young scholarly priest Cayetano was given the charge of exorcising her. The priest had neither faith nor experience in the process of exorcism and he began his treatment with reciting heavenly songs. This was objectionable to other priests and nuns who complained against Cayetano and also against Maria whose unconventional behavior was scandalous. Cayetano was transferred to a leper hospital and Maria was being exorcised in full swing. The inhuman torture inflicted on Maria disturbed the humanist priest Cayetano who began to visit the girl every night and his pity was transformed into an excessive love for the wretched girl. One night after reading out many poems he got exhausted and both of them fell asleep. Next morning he was caught in her cell and he knew that life stopped for them. Here Marquez exposes the cruel remnants of empire, the suffocation of religious superstitions, prejudices and an overall decaying condition that exposes the darkness of mind. It is implied that the real demons lie in the minds of those people who control the society and who have the freedom to accuse anybody of any flaw. The innocent girl Maria could not resist those dangerous demons though she survived the biting of a rabies dog. Thus in all his fictional writings, Marquez's concerns for society are as strong as they are in his journalistic writings.

When viewed from the aspect of the author's social concern and also from that of the narrative style, in some of Marquez's writings the differences between fiction and non-fiction are almost blurred. A real incident in life often forms the background both of his fiction and non-fiction. *Chronicle of a Death Foretold* was based on an event that occurred in the month of January in the year 1951 at Sucre, a small town in Colombia. A medical student Cayetano Gentile Chimento was murdered by Victor Chica Salas for having dishonored Victor's sister who had been returned by her husband. Thirty years later, Marquez published his novel which showing identical fact is a reconstruction of the murder. By the same time two journalists Julio Roca and Camilo Calderon published an exclusive story entitled 'Garcia Marquez to vio morir' (in English translation 'Garcia Marquez saw him Die') in the weekly Colombian magazine *Al Dia* (Bogota, no.1, April 28, 1981). To quote from the Magazine: "In the municipality of Sucre the elders still remember with horror the rainy morning of January 22, 1951, in which a young man from Sucre, Cayetano Gentile Chimento, twenty two years old, medical student at the Javerina university of Bogota and heir of the town's largest fortune, fell butchered by machete, innocent victim of a confused duel of honor, and without knowing for sure why he was dying. Cayetano was killed by Victor and Joaquin Chica Salas, whose sister Margarita, married the previous day with Miguel Reyes Palencia and returned to her family by her husband the same night of the marriage, accused Cayetano of being the author of the disgrace that had prevented her from being a virgin at her marriage." These two journalists ended with the comment that Garcia Marquez enriched and dramatized the facts. They also expressed their hope that their story would help the readers discover for themselves the new elements with which the author had tightly structured his story. In fact readers were puzzled to see whether the book was a piece of investigative journalism or a fiction. For the book is apparently a collection of data from the witnesses to reconstruct a murder that occurred twenty seven years ago. The narrator, a friend of the murdered man, was present in the town during the event, but he did not witness the murder. He starts a fresh investigation based on his own memory and the memory of others in regard to the facts that preceded and followed the murder. As many as thirty seven persons were interviewed by the narrator. He also used several reports which were produced by investigative authorities. The narrator himself describes his effort as "trying to put the broken mirror of memory back together from so many scattered shards" (5). Marquez got amused when the critics were engaged in the search of how much of the novel is based on facts. He is reported to have said in Mexico that the 'drama' in his book was better than the journalistic account of the incident. "The novel appeared on Monday, and a magazine in Bogota had already published a story from the place where the events took place, with photographs of the supposed protagonists. Their job is excellent from a journalistic viewpoint; but it is astonishing that the drama told to the journalists by the witnesses is totally different from that of the novel. Perhaps the word 'totally' is not quite accurate. The point of departure is the same, but the evolution is different. I flatter myself that the drama in my book is better, more controlled, more structured."[3] The author's view on the difference between the journalistic account and the fictionalized account of the same event is once again clarified in the above statement. The journalist has little freedom which is necessary for controlling the outer events while the novelist has full control over his material and only the novelist can twist the facts and mould them to produce a perfect blend of fact and fiction that can satisfy the inquisitive mind. When the incident of murder took place, Marquez was interested in the matter as a journalist. He was then a provincial journalist in a local newspaper which took no interest in the matter and so Marquez could not prepare any journalistic report of the event to get it published. Several years later when he earned fame as a novelist, he started thinking of the incident in literary terms. But his mother opposed the idea of writing a book in which living persons whose mishap was fresh in people's memory would be introduced as characters. Marquez therefore waited a long period of time to start writing a fiction based on the incident of honor killing. And after his novella was published, there was no dearth of critical writing in which the book was compared to the real event in some way or other. In August 1981, a few months after the publication of the book, an article entitled 'The Story of the Story' appeared in Madrid's newspaper *El Pais.* The writer of the article raised question in regard to the authenticity of the reunion of Angela Vicario and Bayardo San Roman, the husband who had returned his wife on the night of their marriage, as shown in the fiction. Marquez declared that his friend Alvaro Cepeda Samudio had given him the information; he quoted his friend and also added his own comment in *El Pais.* Marquez's friend Alvaro was reported to have said to him, "I have a tip for you . . . Bayardo San Roman went back for Angela Vicario. They're living together on Manaure, old and popped out, but happy." And Marquez added his comment: "He did not have to say anything more to make me understand that the end of a long search had arrived. . . . Alvaro Cepeda Samudio's revelation, that Sunday in Sabanilla, made everything fall into place for me. Bayardo San Roman's return to Angela Vicario was undoubtedly, the final missing link. Everything became clear then: because of my fondness for the victim, I had always believed that this was the story of an atrocious crime, when really it must have been the secret history of a terrible love"[4]. But the controversy did not end here. The author was satisfied with the information supplied to him by his friend as the information tallied with his imagination. He needed no further investigation but the journalists continued their search and one of them had an interview with the real husband. It was revealed from this interview that Margarita Chica Salas, the rejected wife in real life, continued to live alone in Sinceligo and her husband, remarried to Enriqueta Obregon, had twelve children with his new wife. Anyway, Garcia Marquez who would interpret this later development as photographic reality from which he always kept his distance is reported to have rejected the entire story of romantic reconciliation of Angela Vicario and Bayardo San Roman and maintained that they did discuss the possibility of reunion, but for reasons of social propriety, remained apart. All this is interesting as Marquez's critics and the common readers too, tended to accept *Chronicle of a Death Foretold* as a piece of journalism while the author created it a fiction. Marquez also used some tricks to create confusion in the minds of his critics in regard to its journalistic nature. Luisa Santiaga is the name of the narrator's mother in the novel; this is the name of Garcia Marquez's mother also in real life and this similarity in names confirms some critics that the narrator is none but Marquez himself. Again, the narrator refers to his proposal of marriage to Mercedes Barcha as soon as she finished primary school (43) and Mercedes Barcha is the name of Marquez's wife, too. A critic Stephen Minta is so confused by this account of the marriage proposal that he fails to decide the exact time of the murder as if it is necessary for evaluating the novel as a work of art.[5]

While the fictional writing *Chronicle of a Death Foretold* looks like a journalistic account of an investigation of a murder, the non-fiction work *The Story of a Shipwrecked Sailor,* for example, have all the qualities of fiction in it. This is the account of a sailor who drifted on a life raft ten days without food and water and was saved by miracle. It is narrated in the first person and ends with the remark, "Some people tell me this story is a fantasy. And I ask them: If it is, then what did I do during my ten days at sea?"(106). This ending is also an authorial trick that creates doubt in the readers' minds in regard to fictional qualities of the work. The author's elaborate introduction to the work entitled 'The Story of This Story,' however, clarifies the background of this non-fiction. The introduction starts with the news of February 28, 1955, that eight crew members of the destroyer 'Caldas' of the Colombian navy had fallen overboard and disappeared during a storm in the Caribbean Sea. The ship was traveling from Mobile Alabama in the United States, where it had docked for repairs, to the Colombian port of Cartagena. A search for the seaman began immediately, with the cooperation of the U.S. Panama Canal Authority, which performs such functions as military control and other humanitarian deeds in the southern Caribbean. After four days the search was abandoned and the lost sailors were officially declared dead. A week later, however, one of them turned up half dead on a deserted beach in northern Colombia, having survived ten days without food or water on a drifting life raft. His name was Luis Alejandro Velasco. The author then declares, "This book is a journalistic reconstruction of what he told me, as it was published one month after the disaster in the Bogota daily *El Espectador.*" The writer then goes on describing that when they tried to reconstruct his adventure minute by minute, neither he nor the sailor knew that the "exhausting digging" would lead them to a new adventure that caused a certain stir in the nation and cost the sailor his honor and could have cost the author his skin. At that time Colombia was under the military dictatorship of General Gustavo Rojas Pinilla, whose two most memorable feats were the killing of students in the center of the capital when the army broke up "a peaceful demonstration with bullets," and the assassination by the secret police of an undetermined number of Sunday bullfight fans who had booed the dictator's daughter at the bullring. The press was censored, and the daily problem for opposition newspapers was "finding politically germ-free stories" with which to entertain their readers.

By this time Garcia Marquez was the staff reporter of *El Espectador* and its director was Gillermo Cano and editor-in-chief, Jose Salgar. The shipwrecked sailor Alejandro Velaso became a celebrity at that time. The armed forces had sequestered him for several weeks in a naval hospital, and he had been allowed to talk only with reporters favorable to the regime and with one opposition journalist who had disguised himself as a doctor. His story had been told piecemeal many times, had been pawed over and perverted, and readers seemed fed up with the hero who had rented himself out to advertise watches (because his watch hadn't even slowed down during the storm); who appeared in shoe advertisements (because his shoes were so sturdy that he had not able to tear them apart to eat them); and who had performed many other publicity stunts. He had been decorated, he had made patriotic speeches on radio, and he had been displayed on television as an example to future generations. He had toured the country amid bouquets and fantasies, signing autographs and being kissed by beauty queens. He also managed to own a small fortune. When such a man came to the office of *El Espectado* uninvited, it was naturally thought that he had hardly anything new to tell, that he was capable of inventing anything for money. He was therefore sent away by others but the director, who caught up with him on the stairway, accepted the deal, and placed him in the hands of Garcia Marquez who wrote, "It was as if he had given me time bomb." The author noted some peculiar qualities in the sailor: he had an exceptional instinct for the art of narration, an astonishing memory and ability to synthesize, and enough uncultivated dignity to be able to laugh at his own heroism. In twenty daily sessions, each lasting six hours, the author took his interview, taking notes and springing trick questions on him to expose contradiction. Finally, they put together an accurate and concise account of his ten days at sea. It was so detailed and so exacting that the author feared that nobody would believe in it. "Not solely for this reason but also because it seemed fitting, we agreed that the story would be written in the first person and signed by him." The surprise occurred during the fourth day of the work when the sailor, asked to give details of the storm that had caused the disaster, answered that there was no storm. It was verified to be true: the weather bureau confirmed that it had been a clear and mild

February in the Caribbean. The truth never published until then, was that the ship, tossed violently by the wind in heavy seas, had spilled its ill-secured cargo and the eight sailors overboard. This revelation meant that three serious offences had been committed: first, it was illegal to transport cargo on a destroyer; second, the overweight prevented the ship from maneuvering to rescue the sailors, and third, the cargo was contraband—refrigerators, television sets, and washing machines. The author writes: "Clearly, the account, like the destroyer, was loaded with an ill-secured moral and political cargo that we hadn't foreseen."

When this account, divided into installments, was published for fourteen consecutive days, it raised a commotion in the country and the Conservative government found it difficult to face the situation. As the truth began to emerge, it would have been politically dishonest to halt publication of the series. The paper's circulation was almost doubled, and there were demands for the back issues as the readers wanted to collect the entire story. "The dictatorship, in accordance with a tradition typical of Colombian governments, satisfied itself by patching up the truth with rhetoric: in a solemn statement, it denied that the destroyer had been loaded with contraband goods." In order to substantiate its charges, the news paper asked the sailor Luis Alejandro Velasco for a list of his fellow crewmen who owned cameras and somehow managed to buy some photographs of the sailors. One week after the publication of the series, the complete story was published in a special supplement illustrated with the sailors' photographs. Behind the groups of friends on the high seas one could see the boxes of contraband merchandise and even, unmistakably, the factory labels. The government was thus fully exposed and turned vindictive. As it was expected from the dictatorial government, it countered the blow with a series of drastic reprisals. Months after, the news paper was shut down and Marquez, who had already been assigned a duty in Italy to get an escape from the revenge of the government, became jobless. And the sailor as he did not recant a word of his story despite the pressure, the threats and the most seductive attempts at bribery, had to leave the Navy, the only career he had, and disappeared into the oblivion of everyday life. To quote from Marquez's introduction, again, "After two years the dictatorship collapsed and Colombia fell to the mercy of other regimes that were better dressed but not much more just, while in Paris I began my nomadic and somewhat nostalgic exile that in certain ways also resembles a drifting raft. No one heard anything more about that lone sailor until a few months later, when a wandering journalist found him seated behind a desk at a bus company. I have seen the photograph taken of him then: he had grown older and heavier, and looked as if life had passed through him, leaving behind the serene aura of a hero who had had the courage to dynamite his own statue." The account was published as book form *The Story of a Shipwrecked Sailor,* fifteen years later and Marquez found it depressing that the publishers were interested not so much in the merit of the story as in the recent fame of its author. This very remark reveals how Marquez was interested in revealing the truth about his country, a country that had been suppressed under different dictatorial rules causing havoc in the lives of common men. For Marquez, truth alone mattered and not the medium of expression. And that is why he hardly bothered if what he wrote was a piece of journalism or a fiction. For in both of these he profusely used the techniques of both.

It is interesting to note that if one compares *Chronicle of a Death Foretold* with *The Story of a Shipwrecked Sailor,* the former may appear as a journalistic writing with however occasional uses of metaphor, simile, hyperbole and symbol, and the latter with its introduction apart, may easily be classified with such works as Yann Montel's *Life of Pi* at least from the viewpoint of a struggle for survival on the wild sea. Take, for example, the description of the search for the necessary files by the narrator in *Chronicle of a Death Foretold* twenty years after the crime: "There was no classification of files whatever and more than a century of cases were piled up on the floor of the decrepit colonial building that had been Sir Francis Drake's headquarter for two days The ground floor would be flooded by high tides and the unbound volumes floated about the deserted offices. I myself did my searching many times with the water up to my ankles in that lagoon of lost causes, and only chance after five years of searching let me rescue some 322 pages filched from the more than 500 that the brief must have had" (99-100). Again, it is reported that the investigating officer was puzzled because of the lack of proof against Santiago Nasar: "On folio 416, in his own handwriting and with thc druggist's red ink, he wrote a marginal note: *Give me a prejudice and I will move the world"* (101). Marquez used the journalistic tricks in order to take the readers to his confidence[6]. Take, again, the fifth section of *The Story of a Ship wrecked Sailor* when after struggling alone on the raft for two days and two nights, his throat dried up and energy lost, the sailor had the hallucination. He closed his eyes and saw his friend Jaime Manjarres, smiling in front of him, holding a plate of fruit and scrambled eggs in his hand. He decided to speak to him and though he did not remember what they talked about he knew that they were talking on deck and suddenly there was the shock of the wave, "the final wave of 11:55," and he woke up with a jolt, holding on the raft with all his strength, lest he fell on the ocean. He claimed that his friend was there and he talked to him and the narration could very well be a part of a fictional writing. "Just before dawn the sky darkened. I was too exhausted even to sleep. Surrounded by darkness, I gave up trying to see the other end of the raft. But I kept peering into the obscurity, attempting to penetrate it. That was when I clearly saw Jaime Manjarres sitting on the gunwale, dressed in his uniform: blue pants and shirt, his cap slightly tilted over the right ear, on which I could clearly read, despite the darkness, "ARC Caldas," "Hello," I said to him, without a start. Undoubtedly Jaime Manjarres was there. Undoubtedly he had always been there. If this had been a dream, it wouldn't have been mattered. But I knew I was fully awake, completely lucid, and I could hear the whistling of the wind and the sounds of the sea, I felt hungry and thirsty. And I hadn't the slightest doubt that Jaime Majarres was with me on the raft. "Why didn't you drink enough water on the ship?" he asked me. "Because we were about to dock at Cartagena," I answered. . . . It was not an apparition. I wasn't afraid. It seemed ridiculous that I had felt lonely before, not realizing that another sailor was on the raft" (40). The sailor's loneliness is best revealed through such hallucinations which could very well be the part of a novel based on shipwreck. Marquez's own words spoken to Peter H. Stone in the 'Paris Review' Interview may be recalled in this context. "I think the influence is reciprocal. Fiction has helped my journalism because it has given it literary value. Journalism has helped my fiction because it has kept me in close relationship with reality."

Marquez claimed that there is no fantasy in his work and that each line he wrote is based on fact. To quote from the 'Parish Review,' again, "It always amuses me that the biggest praise for my work comes for the imagination, while the truth is that there is not a single line in all my work that does not have a basis in reality. The problem is that the Caribbean reality resembles the wildest imagination. . .To find probabilities out of real facts is the work of the journalist and the novelist, and it is also the work of a prophet. The trouble is that many people believe that I'm a writer of fantastic fiction, when actually I'm a very realistic person and write what I believe to be the true socialistic realism." By socialistic realism he did not however mean the meat-and potato realism which was the natural outcome of Western Realistic Novel. Instead, he exposed the root causes of people's sufferings in the Latin American countries and he sincerely believed that unless and until various forms of dictatorship are eradicated, society as a whole has to suffer. Three of his important non-fiction writings—*The Story of a Shipwrecked Sailor* (1970), *Clandestine in Chile* (1986) and *News of a Kidnapping* (1996)—aimed at the exposure of different aspects of misrule and corruption in the functioning of various dictatorial governments in Latin America. *The Story of a Shipwrecked Sailor* exposes the Colombian Government's involvement in using a destroyer for carrying contraband goods—the destroyer *Caldas* of the Colombian navy was "loaded with an ill-secured moral and political cargo"—and it also came out from later investigation that there was illegal business of drugs between the Colombian government and the USA. That a common citizen, a sailor in navy, had to lose his job for telling the truth behind a mishap that had taken the life of his companion sailors is just the tip of the iceberg like corruption. Common citizens cannot feel secured in such a regime. *Clandestine in Chile: The Adventure of Miguel Littin* (Spanish *La Adventura de Miguel Littin Clandestina en chile*) is a thrilling description of how the Chilean film director Miguel Litten, who had been exiled from his land along with five thousand other intellectuals after Augusto Pinochet's coup in 1973, entered Chile in disguise, accompanied by French, Dutch and Italian cinematographers, and was able to complete two documentary films on the functioning of the government, one for cinema and the other for television, exposing thereby the top secret matters, so far kept hidden by the government. Marquez listened to the story of adventure as described by Littin and having based it on an exhaustive interview as well as the documentary films; he prepared the most endearing piece of journalism, tarnishing the Chilean military dictator Augusto Pinochet's reputation. As Marquez wrote in the introduction, some names were changed and many circumstances altered in order to protect the protagonists still living in Chile. He wrote the story in first person as told by Littin to him, trying in that way to preserve his personal and sometimes confidential tone. As he wrote, "By the method of investigation and the character of the material, that is a journalistic report. But it is more, the emotional reconstruction of an adventure whose ultimate result was without doubt warmer and more moving than the original plan, and was successful in making a film exposing the risks of military power." As the book reveals, the author's chief concern is not any personal grudge against Pinochet, but it is a humanist's concern for the wretched condition of the people who are denied the opportunity of a prestigious living in their own land. The title of one chapter 'Those Who Stayed Are Also Exiles' is suggestive enough of the writer's concern for those Chileans who were struggling hard to know the truth but were destined to live under the dictatorial control, secluded both from the past and the present of their land.

News of Kidnapping translated by Edith Grossman, 1997, (Spanish *Noticia de un secuestro,* 1996), is about the drug kingpins who, afraid of being sent to the US, put pressure on the Colombian government through kidnapping ten well known Colombians who were held as hostages. The notorious drug lord Pablo Escobar and his assistants are brilliantly portrayed in this real life tale of suspense. The alternating scenic structure of the work successfully reveals how the dark world of drug cartels works in broad daylight. The lack of good will on the part of the government caused the havoc and the government had little control either over the kidnapper or over the false communiqués. To quote Marquez, "Not knowing what to expect, the presidency alerted the public to a proliferation of false communiqués and asked the people not to put more faith in them than in announcements from the government. But the grave and bitter truth was that the public had implicit trust in the Extraditable communiqués" (38). It is most unfortunate for the public when it has no faith in the functioning of the government as the government has failed to gain the public's confidence. Marquez shows that the complete truth is never known in Colombia, and hence there is no final word on the subject. But the revelation of the horrible experiences of the victims throws light on the insecure condition to which the public in Colombia are destined to live. Thus in his non-fiction writings, all of which may be read as fictional writings, too, Marquez reveals a society in which people are denied the freedom of thought and expression and are destined to suffer from an insecurity and seclusion. In such a society everything is controlled by the unsocial forces, the gentlemen playing the roles of criminals. Common persons are forced to behave as unwanted foreigners in their own land.

Notes

1. George R. McMurry, *Critical Writings on Gabriel Garcia Marquez* (1987; Boston: G.K. Hall).
2. That this assessment was correct is clear from the reaction of the murderers. After they felt themselves safe from the Arabs—Sabtiago Nasar's father being an Arab there was apprehension that the Arab community might take revenge of the murder of Santiago—and were comforted by the honor of having done their duty, they continued to be worried of the persistent smell of blood. "Pedro Vicario couldn't stay there lying on bed, but the same weariness prevented him from standing. The pain in his groin had reached his throat, his urine was shut off, and he suffered the frightful certainty that he wouldn't sleep over again for the rest of his life. . . . He couldn't eat any lunch. Pablo Vicaro, for his part, ate a little bit of everything they brought him, and fifteen minutes later unloosed a pestilential chlorine" (80).
3. Gabriel Garcia Marquez: 'Cronica de una muerte anuncida es mi major novela,' *El Pais* (Madrid, Friday, May 1, 1981; qtd. Jayanti Seth edited *Chronicle of a Death Foretold* (New Delhi: Doaba, 2002), p. 29.
4. Gabriel Garcia Marquez, 'El Cuento del cuento,' *El Pais* (Madrid, August 26, 1981); trans. Gonzalo Diaz-Migoyo in his article,

'Truth Disguised: *Chronicle of a Death (ambiguously) Foretold,'* qtd. Jayanti Seth ed. *Chronicle of a Death Foretold*, pp. 83-99.

5. Stephen Minta expresses his confusion in the following way: "At one point, for example, the narrator mentions his engagement to his future wife Mercedes and refers to their marriage fourteen years later. Since Garcia Marquez and Marcedes Barcha were married in 1958, this would place the of *Chronicle of a Death Foretold* in 1944.Nonetheless, it is clear from other points in the story that the setting must be later—a reference to a time in the past when German knives were unavailable because of the war suggests this, along with a number of other inferences about the age and situation of various characters, There is no point in seeking to resolve those contradictions, for they are deliberately contrived to undermine any sense that the narrator's version of events is somehow more reliable than anyone else's might have been." Qtd. Jayanti Seth, p.103.
6. To quote Marquez's own comments on the tricks of journalistic writing used in fiction:

   Interviewer: You describe seemingly fantastic events in such a minute detail that it gives this their own reality. Is this something you picked up from journalism?

   Marquez: There is a journalistic trick which you can also apply to literature. For example, if you say that there are elephants flying in the sky, people are not going to believe you. But if you say that there are four hundred and twenty five elephants flying in the sky, people will probably believe you. *www.theparisreview.org. /interviews/3196/the art of fiction-69-gabriel-garcia-marquez.*

Appendix

The Art of Garcia Marquez and (Magic) Realism

Though Garcia Marquez's name has been associated with what is commonly called 'magic realism,' he did not use the phrase in connection with his fictional writings. Edith Grossman, who translated several of his works, said in a 2005 interview with Joel Whiting of *Guernica* that "He [Marquez] does not use that term at all, as far as I know. It's always struck me as an easy, empty kind of remark." Some critics like to use Carpentier's phrase *lo real maravilloso* (the marvellous real) instead of 'magic realism' or 'magical realism' in connection with Marquez's fiction. Whichever phrase is used in connection with the narrative art of his fiction, the fact remains that he wholeheartedly opposed the style of European realism, and also the style of psychological novels that prevailed in Europe in the beginning of the twentieth century, and embraced, instead, the one that expands the categories of the real so as to encompass myth, legend, fantastic events and extraordinary experiences of common persons which were excluded by the European masters of realism. He challenged the rationality which is at the root of the Aristotelian concept of Probability and Possibility, a concept that must have been artificial for him as opposed to the real.

A rendering of the impossible and improbable as 'real' brings Marquez close to the Surrealists. Formation of the *Mandragora* group in Chile in 1938 is a proof of the growing popularity of Surrealism in the Latin American countries.

Marquez must have been attracted naturally to Surrealism's emphasis on the absence of all control exercised by reason. The powerful images used in his fiction also remind one of the conviction of the surrealists that the stronger the image the greater its emotional power and poetic reality. But Marquez's whole hearted opposition to dictatorship as revealed in his fictional writings—he used some devices of surrealism along with other devices to render the naked picture of dictatorship—was unique and a similar attempt is not found in the work of any surrealist author. Marquez also felt, as did the surrealists, that ordinary and depictive expressions are vital and important; but in practice the surrealist artists fail to render the ordinary as ordinary and they are often inaccessible while Marquez's priority is accessibility. Surrealist works feature the element of surprise and unexpected juxtaposition; but Marquez seriously attempted to hide all features of surprise in his work and hardly used unexpected juxtaposition for the sake of queer effect. Thus the Surrealists' version of reality is more cerebral and psychological, often exploring the unconscious, while Marquez focuses on the material objects and their actual existence in the world. Fantastic events are rendered by Marquez in an otherwise realistic tone that exposes political realities. Fables, folktales and myths are brought together into contemporary social relevance, as these are brought through the perspectives of the believers.

However, Marquez was not the only author in Latin America to search for an alternative mode of writing fiction. The continent had already developed this new trend, as opposed to the popular Western practice of revealing the 'bourgeois hardship of a mediocre hero' or the stereotyped delineation of the oppression of the poor. It was detected that most of such popularized writings were parts of the program by politically motivated artistic trends. Along with a strong opposition to such trends there was an urge for formal experiments with the genre of fiction. To be specific, the new authors in Latin America sought to present the world around them as if the presuppositions of Western bourgeois society could be erased and a fresh look made possible. Such a fresh look was possible only when reality could be observed through the eyes of those people whose cultural presuppositions were different from those of the Western bourgeois people because of their ethnic origin. To render reality from the perspective of a Cuban black or a Colombian Indian is not just to know the protagonist but to "become" the protagonist in the very act of creation. And to become the protagonist means, first of all, to be a believer in the miracles. Marquez's own words when he recalled how he developed the art of writing a work like *One Hundred Years of Solitude* may be referred to in this context. He said that he followed the technique of his grandmother's story telling who used to describe the most fantastic events without changing her facial expression. Marquez felt that her stories appeared real as she herself believed them to be real. What his grandmother did with her facial expression and her voice, Marquez did with his art of narration so that no one would have any doubt in whatever he narrated. It is a difficult art, no doubt; but he succeeded in conquering the difficulty.

Marquez might have followed his grandmother while describing the fantastic episodes but when he portrays the hard reality—the devastation caused by the authority, for example—he embraced the art of journalism which demands reports in detail along with dispassionate rendering of facts. Symbols are also used profusely to bring the effect of fantasy and they are used as natural happenings. For example, yellow butterflies are perfectly used as symbols of love making in *One Hundred Years of Solitude* and these are also used as links in the plot. After Meme's lover Mauricio Babilonia was driven away by Fernanda, she found the house filled with yellow butterflies (232). When Meme would secretly meet her lover in the bathroom during evening, the house was invaded by yellow butterflies. "Every night on her way back from her bath Meme would find a desperate Fernanda killing butterflies with an insecticide bomb. 'This is terrible,' she would say. 'All my life they told me that butterflies at night bring bad news'"(237).One night, while Meme was in the bathroom, Fernanda went into her bedroom by chance where she found so many butterflies that she could scarcely breathe. She tried to drive those insects away using a piece of cloth and suddenly it occurred to her that there must have been connection between her daughter's going to bathroom and the "mustard plasters that rolled on the floor." She then wasted no time to catch the culprit and punish him. Thus symbols connected with superstitions are used by Marquez for bringing movement in his story. But most often the symbols used in his fiction cannot be interpreted though they add to the effect of 'magic.' To give his account a look of authenticity the author follows the journalistic way of supplying details such as an exact tenure of the continuous rainfall or of continuous lack of rain in the land. The hyperbole used in such descriptions also enhances the 'magical' effect.

The most serious challenge that Marquez had to encounter was the delineation of the history of his land in a 'magical' way. He did it successfully in *One Hundred Years of Solitude* with a grand style with elements taken from legends, myths, folk tales, history, Faulkner's style, Kafka's style and others woven together with his rich imagination. He could detect very well which element would expose the nature of the people of his land. To exhibit the pre-Christian mindset of the ethnic people he thus describes their habit of preserving, and at the time of movement, carrying, the bones of their dear ones after their death. Rebeca in *One Hundred Years of Solitude* brought the bones of her parents with her when she came to stay with the Buendia family in Macondo, and became restless when the bones could not be traced. Erendira's grandmother in 'The Incredible and sad Tale of Innocent Erendira and her Heartless Grandmother' carried with her a box containing the bones of her husband and her son.

To quote Michael Foucault in this context, "Basically it was quite natural that in a time of real belief in the resurrection of bodies and the immortality of the soul, overriding importance was not accorded to the body's remains. On the contrary, from the moment when the people are no longer sure that they have a soul. . .it is perhaps necessary to give much more attention to the dead body which is ultimately the only trace of our existence in the world" (*www.foucault.info/documents/heterotopia.en.html*).

Without any authorial comment on the rituals and beliefs of the ethnic groups Marquez puts forward their practice of carrying the bones of their dead relatives with them while shifting from one place to another and this practice throws much light on their way of life. The ancient history of his land as depicted in his fiction is, above all, the history of the formation of a hybrid race. And the contemporary history is the socio-political history of the land devastated by dictatorial rules and opportunistic foreign organizations. As far as contemporary history is concerned, Marquez must be credited with a rare capacity of preserving data that had been systematically erased by the dictatorial rulers.

Marquez maintained that the style of a fiction is determined by the subject and the mood of the fiction concerned. And that is why the style in his fictional writings varies according to the differences in subject matter and the mood. While the satiric mood of *In Evil Hour* and its theme of political exigencies which make for injustice and corruption require a witty style having superbly placed dialogue and inimitable humor, *No One writes to the Colonel* needs a style fit for its smooth and tender revelation of the underlying pathos. *Autumn of the Patriarch* introduces, through its excessively long sentences, a queer and rather suffocating style for projecting the suffocating condition of the dictatorial rule in postcolonial Colombia. *One Hundred Years of Solitude*, an immensely rich presentation of the history of the land, is written in the grandest style the sweeping brilliance of which has more poetry than prose. Its almost epic grandeur fills the reader's mind with an awe and when the reader completes the novel, he/she is elevated to a position where reality and fantasy are merged together to produce an effect that helps the reader have a total view of life itself on this earth. *Love in the Time of Cholera* written in a strange and brilliant style depicts the varieties of love as scrutinized by the author in a way that could not be imagined earlier. In his other writings too, Marquez changes the style of his writing as per the demand of the theme. In *Clandestine in Chile*, for example, Marquez tells the story plainly in the form of Littin's first-person narrative, as he knew that the story has no need of magical realist embellishment.

One of the most popular writers of the world who received critical acclaim in different corners of the globe, Gabriel Garcia Marquez is one of the successful artists who revolted against the popular British technique of social realism. He paved the way for exposing reality in the socio-political background of postcolonial Latin America and it is rewarding to compare his writings with those of some avant-garde writers of different countries who also sought to break a fresh ground. The Peruvian writer Mario Vergas LIosa's historical novels with their forthright and fascinating reinterpretations of Latin American political upheaval and machinations as well as his delineation of the carnal and passionate adventures of human beings remind one of Garcia Marquez. The Chinese Nobel Laureate Mo Yan's juxtapositions of the horrific and the comic, of shimmering poetry and brutal realism, also come close to some of Marquez's writings. The writer of Indian origin, Salman Rushdie, the owner of Booker's Booker for his *Midnight's Children,* attracted the critics' attention from the moment of the publication of his celebrated novel and *The Times* heralded the book as the second best surprising novel since the publication of *One Hundred Years of Solitude.* It is tempting to conclude with Salman Rushdie's observation on Marquez: "*El realism magical,* magic realism, at least as practiced by Marquez, is a development out of Surrealism that expresses a genuinely 'Third World' consciousness. It deals with what Naipaul has called 'half-made' societies, in which the impossibly old struggles against the appallingly new, in which public corruptions and private anguishes are somehow more garish and extreme than they ever get in the so-called 'North,' where centuries of wealth and power have formed thick layers over the surface of what is really going on. In the works of Marquez, as in the world he describes impossible things happen constantly, and quite plausibly, out in the open under the midday sun. It is a mistake to think of Marquez's literary universe as an invented, self-referential, closed system. He is not writing about Middle earth, but about the one we all inhabit. Macondo exists. That is the magic" (*Imaginary Homelands,* 302).

Bibliography

Apuleyon Mendoza and Garcia Marquez. *The Fragrance of Guava* (Verso, London, 1983).

Bell-Villada, Gene. *Garcia Marquez: The Man and his Work,* (University of North Carolina Press Chapel hill, 1990).

Bloom, Harold Ed., *Gabriel Garcia Marquez* (Chelsea House, New York, 1989).

Dolan Sean: *Gabriel Garcia Marquez* (Chelsea House, New York, 1994).

William, Raymond L.: *Gabriel Garcia Marquez* (Twayne, New York, 1984).

Mc Murray, George R: *Critical Essays on Gabriel Garcia Marquez* (G.K. Hall, Boston, 1987).

Marquez, Gabriel Garcia: *In Evil Hours,* trans. from Spanish by Gregory Rabassa (Picador, 1982i).

_____. *One Hundred Years of Solitude* trans. from Spanish by Gregory Rabassa (Picador, 1982i).

_____. *No One Writes to the Colonel,* trans. from Spanish by J.S. Bernstein, (Harper-Collins, N.Y., 1979).

_____. *The Autumn of the Patriarch,* trans. Gregory Rabassa, (Harper and Row, N.Y., 1976).

_____. *Love in the Time of Cholera,* trans. from Spanish by Edith Grossman (Penguin, 1989i).

_____. *Strange Pilgrims,* trans. Edith Grossman (Penguin, New York, 1994).

_____. *Collected Stories,* trans. Gregory Rabbasa and J.S. Bernstein (Penguin, N.Y., 1996).

_____. *Memoirs of my Melancholy Whores,* trans. from Spanish by Edith Grossman (Jonathan Cape, 2005).

_____. *Chronicle of a Death Foretold,* Trans. from Spanish by Gregory Rabassa (Penguin India, 1996).

_____. *Of Love and Other Demons,* trans. from Spanish by Edith Grossman (Alfred A Knopf, USA, 1994).

_____. *The Story of a Shipwrecked Sailor,* trans. Randolph Hogan (Penguin India, 1996).

_____. *News of a Kidnapping,* trans. Edith Grossman (Penguin, New York, 1997).

_____. *Living to Tell the Tale,* trans. Edith Grossman (Vintage, New York, 2004).

Martin, Gerald. *Gabriel Garcia Marquez, A Life* (Bloomsbury, London, 2008).

Rushdie, Salman. *Imaginary Homelands, Essays and Criticism 1981-1991* (Vintage, London, 2010).